Tai Ji Bing Shu

Chen Kung Series
From the Private Family Records of Master Yang Luchan

Volume Six

Tai Ji Bing Shu

太極兵術

Discourses on the Taijiquan
Weapon Arts of Sword, Saber, and Staff

A New and Revised Edition
of *T'ai Chi Sword, Sabre & Staff*

Translation and Commentary
by Stuart Alve Olson

Valley Spirit Arts
Phoenix, Arizona

Translations from *Tai Ji Quan, Sword, Saber, Staff, and Dispersing Hands Combined* by Chen Kung (太極拳刀劍桿散手合編, 陳公著, *Tai Ji Quan Dao Jian Gan San Shou He Lun, Chen Gong Zhe*).

Disclaimer

Please note that the author and publisher of this book are NOT RESPONSIBLE in any manner whatsoever for any injury that may result from practicing the techniques and/or following the instructions given within. Since the physical activities described herein may be too strenuous in nature for some readers to engage in safely, it is advised that a physician be consulted before training.

Copyright © 2014 by Stuart Alve Olson.

Originally published by Bubbling-Well Press in 1986 as *T'ai Chi Sword, Sabre & Staff*. Reprinted by Valley Spirit Arts in 2012 to 2013. Second Edition published in 2014. All rights reserved. No part of this book may be reproduced or used in any form or by any means, electronic or mechanical, including photocopying, recording, or by any information storage and retrieval system, without prior written permission from Valley Spirit Arts.

Library of Congress Control Number: 2014934345
ISBN-13: 978-1-889633-17-6
ISBN-10: 1-889633-17-8

Valley Spirit Arts, LLC
Manager: Lily Shank
Series Editor: Patrick Gross
www.valleyspiritarts.com
contact@valleyspiritarts.com

In loving memory of Taijiquan
Master T.T. Liang
梁東材太極拳師
(1900 to 2002)

**The Immortal Ancestor Zhang Sanfeng
Founder of Taijiquan**

A statue in his honor at Wu-Dang Temple,
Wu-Dang Mountain, Hubei Province, China.

Yang Family Lineage

Yang Style Founder, Yang Luchan
陽露禪
(1799–1872)

Yang Banhou
陽班侯
(1837–1892)
Son of Yang Luchan

Yang Jianhou
陽健侯
(1842–1917)
Son of Yang Luchan

Yang Shaohou
陽少侯
(1862–1930)
Son of Jianhou

Yang Chengfu
陽澄甫
(1883–1936)
Son of Jianhou

Contents

Zhang Sanfeng x
Biography of Master Chen Kung xii
Introduction 1

Tai Ji Sword, Saber, and Staff

Section One: Tai Ji Sword 7
  Chen Kung's Introduction 7
  Tai Ji Sword Praise 13
  Tai Ji Sword Form Instructions 14
  List of Tai Ji Sword Form Postures 104

Section Two: Tai Ji Saber 107
  Chen Kung's Introduction 107
  Tai Ji Saber Praise 112
  Tai Ji Saber Form Instructions 115
  List of Tai Ji Saber Form Gestures 161

Section Three: Tai Ji Binding Staff 163
  Chen Kung's Introduction 163
  Single-Person Binding Staff Method 168
    First Solo Drill: Kai, He, and Fa 169
    Second Solo Drill: Bo, He, and Fa 172

Two-Person, Level-Circular Sticking and Adhering
Binding Staff 178
    Jabbing the Shoulder 178
    Jabbing the Leg 180
        Fixed Stance Drill 180
        Active-Step Drill 181
Two-Person, Fixed Standing Circular Form, Sticking
and Adhering Binding Staff Method 183
Two-Person, Active-Step, Four Staff Methods
of Jabbing the Heart, Leg, Shoulder, and Throat 186
    Jabbing the Heart 187
    Jabbing the Leg 188
    Jabbing the Shoulder 189
    Jabbing the Throat 190
List of Tai Ji Binding Staff Forms 192

About the Translator 193
About the Publisher 201
About the Sanctuary of Dao 202

Zhang Sanfeng

Song Dynasty Immortal Ancestor and Founder of Taijiquan

Painting of Zhang Sanfeng watching a bird attacking a snake from his meditation hut on Wu-Dang Mountain, Hubei Province.

From the simple event of watching a bird attacking a snake, Master Zhang formulated the basic premises for the practice of Taijiquan.

As the snake evaded the strikes of the bird's beak and wings, Master Zhang noticed that it would coil and twist away when attacked. When the bird struck the snake's tail, the snake's head would immediately respond. If the bird then attacked the head, the snake's tail would respond. And when the bird resorted to assaulting the snake's body, its head and tail both responded.

After several failed attempts to defeat the snake, the bird surrendered and flew away.

From observing the snake, Zhang concluded that employing the entire body as one unit was more powerful than just moving the arms or legs independently, being pliable and relaxed meant greater efficiency and endurance of movement, and that the yielding can overcome the unyielding.

From the insights acquired in watching the bird and snake, Zhang was inspired to create the Thirteen Postures of Taijiquan.

Zhang Sanfeng is also credited with writing the *Tai Ji Quan Treatise* (太極拳論, *Tai Ji Quan Lun*,[1] and *Tai Ji Secret Arts of Refining the Elixir of Immortality* (太極煉丹秘訣, *Tai Ji Lian Dan Bi Jue*).[2] This later book is one of the best internal alchemy works in Chinese, wherein his meditation methods, especially, are very effective and adaptable to modern culture.

1. See *Tai Ji Quan Treatise: Attributed to the Song Dynasty Daoist Priest Zhang Sanfeng* (Valley Spirit Arts, 2011) for a fuller biography of Zhang Sanfeng and a translation of this text.
2. See *Refining the Elixir: The Internal Alchemy Teachings of Daoist Immortal Zhang Sanfeng* (Valley Spirit Arts, 2014).

Biography of Master Chen Kung

Born in 1906, Master Chen Kung (a.k.a., Yearning K. Chen and Chen Yen-lin) passed away in Shanghai, China, in 1980. His book *Tai Ji Quan Sword, Saber, Staff, and Dispersing Hands Combined* revolutionized many aspects of Taijiquan practice and theory, especially those concerning his discourses on Intrinsic Energy (勁, Jin), Sensing Hands (推手, Tui Shou), Greater Rolling-Back (大 攦, Da Lu), and Dispersing Hands (散手, San Shou). His explanations of intrinsic energies had never before appeared in any previous Taijiquan-related book, which really made him and his work an enigma.

In 1978, Master Jou Tsung-hwa met with him in Shanghai and reported that Chen started practicing Taijiquan at age four and was a doctor of Chinese medicine.

Around 1930, Chen Kung, a rich merchant and student of Yang Chengfu (陽澄甫) asked to borrow the family transcripts for just one evening so that he might read them to enhance his practice. Chen had been a loyal and dedicated student, so Yang Chengfu consented, knowing that in one night it would be difficult for even a fast reader to finish the book. What Yang didn't know was that Chen had hired seven transcribers to work through the night to copy the entire work. After Chen's disappearance (around 1932) he changed professions from merchant to doctor of Chinese medicine. During that year portions of the manuscript started appearing in various journals, which infuriated the Yang family.

Later, in 1943, Chen's entire copied notes appeared in book form and enjoyed rapid sales throughout China. This further infuriated the Yang family, who then released their own book claiming that Chen's publication was a forgery and that their new, smaller work was the genuine material. Chen, in typical Chinese fashion, claimed his book contained his own theories and that he only used the Yang family name for authenticity. This was Chinese politics at its best.

Master Liang told me this story. He had heard it through his teacher Prof. Cheng Man-ch'ing who heard it from his teacher, Yang Chengfu. With this kind of oral testimony I was never sure about the details. However, Master Jou Tsung-hwa said that Chen Kung confirmed the story when they met in 1978, and now Donald Chen, Chen Kung's grandson, confirmed it to me as well.

Before anyone accuses Chen of any wrongdoing, clearly the Taijiquan world owes him a great debt, whatever the ethics or politics that were involved. The Yang family teachings might well have remained hidden or become lost; likewise, the Yang family might never have published the various works of their own. An even greater result was that many masters, for whatever reasons, began publishing their works as well. Chen's courage created a chain reaction of teachers going public with their knowledge.

In 1947, Chen Kung's *Tai Chi Ch'uan: Its Effects and Practical Applications* appeared from Willow Pattern Press in Shanghai, China. The book lists Yearning K. Chen as the author and Kuo Shuichang as the translator. The interesting thing about this book is that it doesn't appear to be wholly derived from the original 1943 Chinese version of Chen Kung's work used with my present translation. The chapters on physics, psychology, and morality included in the English edition make it completely distinct from the text I used for the series. The solo form instructions and practical application explanations are similar to the 1943 Chinese text, but the two are not identical by any other means, and it did not include the discourses on intrinsic energies as presented in *Tai Ji Jin*.

Introduction

This book was first published in 1986 under the title *Tai Chi Sword, Sabre & Staff*. Since that time I have received many requests to republish it, but (like the other books in the Chen Kung Series) I have waited until I could re-edit and revise the material as a whole. Finally, with the help of my partners at Valley Spirit Arts, and the support of many students, we are completing the entire Chen Kung Series, first by updating the previously published books and then including new volumes of material I have previously never released. When we started this project in 2013, I thought we could complete the series in six volumes, but it now looks like it will take seven or eight.

The volumes are ordered, in part, to correspond with Chen Kung's book, but also to show a type of progression for learning. Meaning, ideally, a student would start out learning the Taiji Qigong form, then progress to the solo form and two-person training, and then to the weapons. However, Master Liang always taught everything at the same time, because no matter what aspect of Taijiquan one starts with they all relate to each other. I have learned many things from training the weapons that helped with my solo form, and vice versa.

By the time the whole series is published and you have become familiar with the complete system of Taijiquan training, you will also see how it is less about progressing from one form of exercise to another, than about integrating all the methods, principles, and teachings into one complete art.

Although this book is the sixth volume in the series, it is being published before volumes three to five because it was one of the original four volumes published previously. That said, however, I have thoroughly gone over the text to include the Chinese and Pinyin, as well as ensure that it stays faithful to Chen Kung's Chinese work. Like the other books in the series, we are using Chen Kung's original line art, and saving some of the instructional/demonstration work for teachers and students to show in the companion DVDs.

This new edition of *Tai Ji Bing Shu* is not only a worthwhile update to the previous edition, but it far surpasses it in scope and appearance. Although the discourses on Tai Ji Sword, Saber, and Staff comprise the final section of Chen Kung's Chinese text, this was actually the first section that Master Liang encouraged me to translate way back in the 1980s, so I know how important he considered the learning of them.

The popularity of this section of Chen Kung's text within the Taijiquan community has been widespread, even being published in Chinese as a separate work. I hope that it will share the same respect and popularity in English as it has in Chinese.

Most modern Taijiquan practicers overlook the importance of training weapons—even considering them instruments of violence. The premise for Taijiquan weapon training, however, has more to do with developing intrinsic energy (勁, jin, see *Tai Ji Jin,* volume 2 in the Chen Kung Series, for more information) than with training the techniques and use of weapons for self-defense.

Sword training (the double-edged weapon) develops not only heightened focus (an aspect of the spirit), but also the skill of extending the intrinsic energy through the hands and arms. The footwork for the sword relates to stepping methods of Eight

Diagram Palms (八卦掌, Ba Gua Zhang), as it relies on the Ba Stance *(Ba,* 八, being the character for eight in Chinese). The sword is the most refined of all Tajiiquan weapons and practices. Wielding a sword is comparable to using a Chinese writing brush, as the yin and yang aspect of energy must be expressed in the hands and fingers. The manipulation of the double-edged sword must be relaxed and precise.

Saber training (single-edged sword, or long knife) develops the strength of the spine and the skill of issuing the qi from the spine. It also aids in learning to relax the shoulders. The footwork for saber relates to stepping methods of Mind-Intent Form Fists (形意拳, Xing-Yi Quan), as it relies heavily on slide stepping (third-step, wherein the rear foot slides forward when issuing energy) and Seven Star stances (where the front-foot toes are raised, used to sweep the back of an opponent's leg or foot). The saber makes use of a more expansive energy than that of the double-edged sword, as the energy applied to it is considerably stronger and more energetic.

Staff focuses on the development of the waist and the skill of directing the intrinsic energy through the waist. The staff is the most powerful of all Taijiquan weapons. The resulting skill of Issuing energy is greatly enhanced through training of the staff. It is the most Taijiquan-like weapon in that the waist must be exclusively used to wield the staff. The footwork in Tai Ji Binding Staff is taken from the Taijiquan solo form, as it relies heavily on the Bow Stance (one foot in front, the other in the rear—like an archer standing to shoot an arrow). The Yang family Binding Staff drills and exercises are actually spear techniques, which is why the Binding Staff in application is single ended. After a tragic accident resulted in the death of Yang Banhou's daughter during spear practice, the spear tips were removed and the methods adapted to the staff. This is why no double-ended staff techniques are found within the Yang family training, unlike other staff kung fu systems.

The sword and saber instructions contained here are for solo practice only, but the staff instructions contain both solo drills and two-person exercises. Although there are two-person training forms for sword and saber, they are not part of Chen Kung's original work.

Republishing this book has been a pleasure. Not only because it is one volume closer to the completion of the entire Chen Kung Series, but also because it is important to present the weapon usage within Taijiquan. The sword, saber, and staff are complete systems of Taijiquan practice in themselves. Almost all information presently published about Taijiquan relates mainly to the empty-hand solo form practice. The weapons of Taijiquan are not vehicles for violence, but rather for the discipline, extension, and expression of intrinsic energy. The Chinese learned long ago the knowledge rooted in the use of the writing brush—that when given an object or tool with which to focus the mind, people can find not only tranquility but their true self as well. The sword, saber, and staff have proven to be excellent tools with which to accomplish this goal.

It is my hope that all practicers of Taijiquan or other martial arts and health regimes open up to the possibility of training one or more of these incredible instruments.

—Stuart Alve Olson

Tai Ji Sword, Saber, and Staff

太極劍刀桿

Section One

Tai Ji Sword

太極劍

Chen Kung's Introduction[1]

Tai Ji Jian [Supreme Ultimate Double-Edged Sword], also known as Tai Ji Thirteen Posture Sword, has the following thirteen secret characters [meanings]:[2]

1.	Chou	抽	(Lashing)
2.	Dai	帶	(Carrying)
3.	Ti	提	(Raising)
4.	Ge	格	(Blocking)
5.	Ji	擊	(Piercing)
6.	Ci	刺	(Stabbing)
7.	Dian	點	(Pointing)
8.	Beng	崩	(Snapping)
9.	Jiao	攪	(Stirring)
10.	Ya	壓	(Pressing)
11.	Pi	劈	(Splitting)
12.	Jie	截	(Intercepting)
13.	Xi	洗	(Clearing)

The venerable members of the Yang family were the first Taijiquan authors to hand down the names of these sword skills. The sword form postures are extremely beautiful to watch, and the applications are profound and wonderful.

To master these movements, you must have a nimble waist and agile legs. The principles governing the sword postures are similar to those of Taijiquan. To properly perform these movements, it is essential to retain a light and sensitive energy on top of the head, hollow the chest and straighten the back, sink the shoulders and lower the elbows, relax the waist, and make the wrists flexible. Also, you must sink the qi to the Dan Tian and issue the intrinsic energy [jin] from the spine.

The sword postures can be easily learned, but are very difficult to master. Ordinarily, those who begin studying never acquire any really profound skill because they practice recklessly; the majority quit because outwardly their postures lack beauty and grace. This is because their waist and legs are not nimble. As a result they do not comprehend the practical uses of the sword postures.

For the sake of those who wish to pursue and acquire a genuine understanding of both practice and application, I have compiled this material. But, before describing the unique Taijiquan sword movements and practical uses, I must summarize some of the orthodox principles. Additionally, I wish to elucidate that one pursues this as an art, and because there is a very narrow path to follow, prevention must be taken to avoid going astray.

Moreover, the sword itself has two blade edges. (It is best to do away with the sharp blade edges.) Properly, one edge should not be distinguishable from the other. Either edge can be used and both are normally unusually sharp. Under no circumstances should the sword edges be pulled or drawn by the hands, placed too near the body, twisted about the head,[3] or be obstructive to the waist as, by doing so, it will not be the opponent who gets injured, but yourself. Therefore, when actually employing the sword it is absolutely essential that the entire body be light and spirited. The head must be held up as if suspended from above. You should breathe in a natural manner and direct the eyes to the sword tip, so that the essence of your spirit is in harmony with the sword, so the sword and practitioner become one.

When gripping the sword, you must be gentle, relaxed, and nimble. Avoid gripping the sword too tightly with the hand or fingers, as this is really detrimental to the application. Only three fingers are needed to hold the sword: thumb, middle, and ring fingers. The index and little fingers are usually held in a loose and relaxed manner [away from the sword handle]. The palm is empty, just like that of holding a Chinese writing brush.

The internal intrinsic energy is directed up into the Dan Tian and moved through the sword. It is issued from the spine, through the arm, and into the sword tip. This instant of issuing energy is like that of shooting an arrow: it moves resolutely, straight ahead.

Wielders of the sword move in a very subtle manner and become, themselves, the sword. This is true mastery! At this point, they will have total concentration and reach a level of transformation. This is called the "wonderful use of the sword." It takes a long time, however, to successfully learn the sword methods so that the sword can be utilized effectively.

The most called upon point of reference for striking an opponent is the hand (or wrist) with which they engage their weapon. Upon having their wrist cut, an opponent must try to maintain control of their weapon or become defenseless.

Tai Ji Bing Shu: Discourses on the Taijiquan Weapon Arts

In ancient times, the swords first used by adepts were twenty-three inches in length. The sword tip and edges were extraordinarily sharp. That made it possible to slash an opponent's wrist, pierce their heart, or stab their knee.

You must also pay proper attention to the sword guard knob. It is essential that the hand be constantly separated from the back of the guard knob and not pass beyond it [onto the blade].

It is commonly said: "With a single-edged knife one observes the handle, but with a double-edged sword one observes the guard knob."

Those who learn and understand this will avoid great error.

—Chen Kung

Translator's Notes

1. In all volumes of the series, Chen Kung's text appears in this typeface. My translator's notes [and bracketed comment's within Chen Kung's text] appear in this font.

   Not all Chinese names are represented in Pinyin. This is out of respect to certain people who styled their names according to the Wade-Giles system. Also, I prefer to style the term "gong fu" in the older and more recognizable form of "kung fu."

   I avoid using Tai Ji (or Taiji) on its own to describe any practice within the art of Taijiquan (or Tai Ji Quan). "Tai Ji" is a philosophical term adopted from *The Book of Changes* (易經, *Yi Jing*) by Zhou Dunyi (1017–1073 CE), a neo-Confucian who invented the Tai Ji Symbol

(☯) or "yin-yang" symbol. "Taijiquan" is more accurate in describing this art of health, self-defense, wisdom, and immortality.

Tai Ji (Supreme Ultimate), then, should always appear in conjunction with some aspect of the art, such as in Tai Ji Qigong, Tai Ji Tui Shou (Sensing Hands), Tai Ji Sword, Tai Ji Solo Form, and so on, to distinguish it from its philosophical meaning.

2. The meanings and uses of the "thirteen secret characters" are presented within the instructions of the sword postures themselves. The applications of the thirteen characters within the sword methods are quite varied, just as the Taijiquan Thirteen Posture secret meanings are applied and used in the empty-hand form. These secret meanings run from coarse applications to the very subtle, and are correlated with the Thirteen Postures of Taijiquan (see list below). As in Taijiquan, the Five Operations (correlations of the Five Elements) of Advancing, Withdrawing, Looking-Left, Gazing-Right, and Central Equilibrium are aspects of how the Eight Postures (or operations) function. So Warding-Off (or Lashing) can function with any of the Five Operations, and this is true for the other seven postures: Rolling-Back (Carrying), Pressing (Raising), Pushing (Blocking), Pulling (Piercing), Splitting (Stabbing), Elbowing (Pointing), and Shouldering (Snapping).

As with the Thirteen Postures of Taijiquan it is not a simple matter of looking at or describing the thirteen

secret characters as purely individual techniques. The following list shows the relationship between the Thirteen Postures and the Tai Ji Jian thirteen secret characters:
1. Warding-Off relates with Lashing.
2. Rolling-Back with Carrying.
3. Pressing with Raising.
4. Pushing with Blocking.
5. Pulling with Piercing
6. Splitting with Stabbing.
7. Elbowing with Pointing.
8. Shouldering with Snapping.
9. Advancing with Stirring.
10. Withdrawing with Pressing.
11. Looking-Left with Splitting.
12. Gazing-Right with Intercepting.
13. Central Equilibrium with Clearing.

So, in looking at the correlations, you can deduce that Lashing, for example, can function in the operations of either Stirring, Pressing, Splitting, Intercepting, and Clearing (which equate with the Five Operations of body movements).

3. Twisting or running the sword edge over the head is considered to be an act of severing the spirit, the etheric connection of the human body with Heaven.

Tai Ji Sword Praise

From the beginning, the way of the sword
has been difficult to hand down.

Like a dragon or a rainbow,
it is subtle and abstruse.

Should it be used like that of
a hacking knife?

The old sword immortal Sanfeng
would die of laughter.

Tai Ji Sword Form Instructions

1. Beginning Posture
起势, Qi Shi
Face North[1]

Posture Instructions
Place the feet evenly apart in an open, fixed stance. This stance is identical to the beginning posture of Taijiquan.

Hold the right palm face down and extend the fingers out to the front. The left hand holds the sword. Grasp the sword handle

with the thumb, middle, and ring fingers and place the index finger along the sword handle so that it points toward the sword's guard knob. Relax the little finger and allow it to hang loosely. Hold the spine of the sword blade along the left arm, but do not hold the sword directly against the arm. (See Illustration #1.)

Internal Instructions
Relax the waist and coccyx.
Let the entire body be tranquil so the spirit [神, shen] will unfold.
Center the qi [氣] between the chest and abdomen.

Calmly sink the qi into the Elixir Field [丹田, Dan Tian, lower abdomen], so that the Spirit of Vitality [精神, Jing Shen] can be aroused into action.

Imagine the head is being held upward as if by a string [from the Hundred Returns (百會, Bai Hui) point on top of the head].

The spirit of the eyes gazes directly forward.

Chen Kung's Comment

When holding the sword, do not press it to the backside of the arm too firmly because the weapon may have extra sharp edges. Being even a little careless can cause injury.

Translator's Note

1. Chen Kung did not include directional references in his text. Instead, he used "front," "left," "right," "diagonal," and so on, which are not always clear. This is why all the directional references at the beginning of each posture as well as within the posture instructions appear in brackets or in my commentary font. Directions at the beginning of each posture indicate where the posture ends. Since I added the directions, just assume that whatever direction you are facing when you start the exercise is "north." This applies to saber and any of the other Taijiquan forms, as the directions provide a frame of reference and don't need to be taken literally.

2. Step Forward and Unite the Sword Posture
上步合劍式,
Shang Bu He Jian Shi
Face North

Posture Instructions
(Face towards the front.) Raise the left leg and bend the knees equally. Move both hands simultaneously back, keeping them at shoulder width as they move.

上步合劍式 (2)

    Step forward with the left foot one step. The right foot follows. With the legs bent, seat the waist so that the whole body is in a low squatting position. The two arms press forward and simultaneously unite in front; the two fingers of the right hand, index and middle, cross over and touch the back of the left wrist. (See Illustration #2.)

Internal Instructions
Hold the body upright as if suspended from above.
Hollow the chest and raise the back.
Draw in the Tail Gateway [尾路, Wei Lu].
The body is kept in a low squatting position.
Mobilize the intrinsic energy without the slightest interruption.
The spirit of the eyes gazes directly forward.

Application

This posture is just like the previous *Beginning Posture*. It is only a ceremonial movement.

3. The Immortal Guiding the Road
仙人指路,
Xian Ren Zhi Lu
Face West

路指人仙 (3)

Posture Instructions

(Face towards the left.) Both hands follow the waist and legs in turning towards the right. The right hand circles upward until it reaches the side of the right ear. The left hand circles to the right side of the body. The body rises slightly.

Turn the waist to the left and step out at an angle with the left foot in the leftward direction so that the foot points forward [west]. Bend the knee and seat it firmly.

Simultaneously, the left hand turns until it reaches the left side of the pelvis. The two fingers of the right hand, middle and index, extend outward as they follow the circling gesture of the waist. The Tiger's Mouth [虎口, Hu Kou, qi center in the fleshy area between the thumb and index finger] faces upward.

Gradually straighten the right leg. The legs finish in a Bow Stance. (See Illustration #3.)

Internal Instructions

Do not stoop the body forward.

Suspend the head from above so that the tailbone is positioned correctly, but do not straighten or stretch it upwards too much.

The tip of the right elbow hangs downward slightly.

Sink the two shoulders.

The spirit of the eyes gazes directly forward.

Application

The two fingers of the right hand are used to induce [引, yin][2] the opponent or to point [點, dian] a pulse.

Translator's Note

2. *Yin* is one of the intrinsic energies of Taijiquan, and means to "provoke, entice, or induce" an opponent. The *two fingers* refers to using the Sword Charm (劍符, Jian Fu). In this position, the hand's index and middle fingers are extended (like a sword) with the ring and little fingers folded into the palm of the hand and held by the thumb (as you would in making a fist). The sword charm is used for striking qi points (referred to as "pointing," *dian*) on an opponent's body. Yin, then, is kind of like a warning or threat of striking a vital point, and dian (pointing) is the actual striking. The pointing (or striking) of a vital point is quite serious, so the use of yin (induce) is normally applied first.

4. Triple Bracelets Encircling the Moon

三還套月, San Huan Tao Yue

Face West

Part One

Posture Instructions

(一) 月套環三 (4)

(Face towards the left.) Lift up the right foot and step forward with a crosswise step, putting it down with the tip of the foot facing towards the right [north] and the heel towards the left. Bend the legs to lower the body into a squatting position. At the same time raise the left hand [holding the sword] upwards at an angle until it is level with the chest. This motion is a pushing gesture [meaning, it is like using Pushing energy in the Taijiquan solo form]. Direct the bottom of the sword handle forward and then back in a half circling movement. Maintain a bend in the left elbow. The back of the left hand faces upward, with the palm edge facing outward. The right palm turns over so that it faces upward. Finish with the left hand in front and the right hand behind. (See Illustration #4.)

Internal Instructions
Retain a light energy on top of the head.
Hollow the chest and raise the back.
Sink the shoulders and suspend the elbows.
Draw in the Tail Gateway.
Do not drop the body into too low of a position or bend forward too far.
The spirit of the eyes gazes directly forward.

Application
With the left hand holding the sword, push forward to block [格, ge] the opponent's wrist or body.

Part Two
[Face North]
(Face towards the front.)
Continue to lower the body into a low squatting position by further bending the legs. Sit on the right leg with the left heel raised. When moving downward, the fingers of the right hand face outward as the arm follows the dropping gesture. At the same time the left hand moves outward to a position level with the shoulder, with the sword placed along the left arm. Do not

（二）月套璟三（5）

Section One: Tai Ji Sword

press it against the arm. The body turns to the right, although the direction is still to the front [north]. (See Illustration #5.)

Internal Instructions
Suspend the head from above to position the tailbone correctly.
Do not lean forward.
Sink the two shoulders evenly.

Application
The fingers of the right hand can be used to either induce [引, yin] the opponent or to point [點, dian] a pulse.

Part Three
[Face West]
(Face towards the left.) The body rises as the legs straighten. The left foot then steps in the [westward] direction. Bend the left knee and seat it firmly. Straighten the right leg with the feet finishing in a Bow Stance.

The two hands simultaneously move inward levelly. The right hand goes left [west] and the left hand goes right

(三) 月套環三 (6)

Tai Ji Bing Shu: Discourses on the Taijiquan Weapon Arts

[east]. The hands unite, with the right hand grasping the sword handle. (See Illustration #6.)

Internal Instructions
Slightly curve the hands and arms.
Suspend the head to straighten the body.
Draw in the Tail Gateway.
The spirit of the eyes gazes directly to the front.

Application
The right hand retrieves the sword.

5. Major Star of the Dipper
大魁星,
Da Kui Xing
Face West

Posture Instructions
(Face towards the left.) The right hand takes hold of the sword. Next, the waist and legs make a rightward turning gesture as the body moves downward towards the right and rear. Bend the right leg as the weight shifts to it (changing it to substantial). The sword follows the waist

movement of this rightward gesture. Stir up [撹, jiao] to the opponent's knee when the movement is just about completed by turning over the wrist as the sword reaches the [northeast] corner. The right hand Tiger's Mouth faces up.

The body now turns left [west], as the left leg raises (the foot points directly down and the thigh is held levelly). Raise the sword tip until it is by the head area. Facing left [west] stab [刺, ci] levelly and bend the right arm.

Simultaneously, the two fingers of the left hand, middle and index, extend forward [west]. Slightly bend the right knee and lower the body into a slight squatting position. (See Illustration #7.)

Internal Instructions
Clearly distinguish between the substantial and insubstantial aspects.
Suspend the head and draw in the Tail Gateway.
Do not stoop forward or look upwards.
Keep the body centered and upright.
The spirit of the eyes gazes directly to the front.

Application
When turning to the back [northeast], first attack the opponent's knee. When returning the body to an upright position [and facing west], stab [刺, ci] levelly at the opponent's throat or attack their wrist. The two fingers of the left hand strike [點, dian] the opponent's pulse[3] [穴道, xue dao].

Translator's Note

3. The Sword Charm (劍符, Jian Fu) is held diagonally upward in Taiji Sword. Holding it directly out is considered too impolite and confrontational. Also, the Sword Charm in Taiji Sword is potential, not kinetic, so this is more of a reserve position. Chen's reference to the *xue dao* (pulse) means that the Sword Charm can be directed to strike (point, 點, dian) a qi center along a meridian of the opponent's body.

6. The Swallow Searches for Water
燕子抄水,
Yan Zi Chao Shui
Face West

水 抄 子 燕 (8)

Posture Instructions
(Face towards the left.) The sword turns right then goes back [to the northeast]; from above, split [劈, pi] downward until reaching the level of the shoulder.

The left hand simultaneously, remaining on line with the shoulder, presses forward [west].

Step out to the left with the left foot. Bend the leg and seat it firmly. Straighten the right leg; the legs finish in a Bow Stance facing toward the left front side [west].

The sword, following the waist and legs, circles to the front [north] then moves to the diagonal back left side [southwest] as it strikes levelly. Simultaneously, place the left two fingers on the right Pulse Gate[4] [脉門, Mo Men, aka Door of the Pulses]. (See Illustration #8.)

Internal Instructions
The sword tip points upward.
Suspend the head so that the body is upright.
Draw in the Tail Gateway.
Fix your gaze on the tip of the sword.

Application
First split [劈, pi] in the rear direction at the incoming opponent. When returning [to the west], carry [帶, dai] to the opponent's wrist (perhaps following a strike or a stab [刺, ci]). After carrying, turn over [your] wrist and with a crosswise striking motion, sever the opponent's head.

Translator's Note
4. The Pulse Gate (脉門, Mo Men) is where the hand meets the wrist, area used for checking the pulses in Chinese medicine.

7. Obstruct and Sweep, Right and Left
左右攔掃, Zuo You Lan Sao
Face West

Part One, Right Obstruct and Sweep

Posture Instructions
(Face towards the left.) Step diagonally to the right [northwest] with the right foot. Bend the right leg and seat it firmly. Straighten the left leg gradually.

Following this, the waist and legs turn towards the right as the body moves into a low squatting position. At the same time turn over

掃 攔 右 (9)

the right wrist so it is face down and begin to move the sword to the right at the level of the right knee.

The left hand simultaneously goes back after it loses contact with the right wrist. The upper body faces slightly to the right at an angle, stooping a little to the front. (See Illustration #9.)

Section One: Tai Ji Sword

Internal Instructions
Suspend the head from above so that the body is upright.
Relax the waist and pelvis.
Turn the body only partially to the front.
Do not use intrinsic energy, as this gesture involves only
　　a minor slicing action and do not hold the sword blade
　　too low.
Gaze at the sword blade.

Application
The application for this posture joins with the previous posture *The Swallow Searches for Water*. Strike the back of an opponent's wrist and when they pull back, follow this movement by stepping forward to the right and levelly intercepting [截, jie] their knee.

Part Two, Left Obstruct and Sweep
[Face West]
(Face towards the left.) Step diagonally to the left [southwest] with the left foot. Bend the left knee and seat it firmly. Gradually straighten the right leg.

　　Simultaneously, the right hand moves towards the left. As it moves, turn the wrist

抁　攔　左 (10)

upward. The sword tip faces upward. Following this, turn the waist and legs towards the left and the body drops into a low squatting position.

As the sword moves towards the left, it slices [截, jie, intercepting] levelly (on line with the waist). At the same time the left hand rises above the forehead. The upper body is now facing slightly to the left at an angle and a little forward. (See Illustration #10.)

Internal Instructions
The sword should go out levelly, but neither too high
    nor too low.
The spirit of the eyes gazes levelly.
This is just like the previous posture of *Obstruct and Sweep*,
    Right Style.

Application
The application for this posture is joined with the previous right style of *Obstruct and Sweep*. Intercept [截, jie] to the back of the opponent's wrist when moving right; yield and neutralize. You must then continue with this gesture by stepping forward and to the left. When turning to face the opponent, intercept [截, jie] levelly to their waist region.

8. Minor Star of the Dipper
小魁星,
Xiao Kui Xing
Face Southwest

星 魁 小 (11)

Posture Instructions
(Face towards the left diagonal direction.) With the right hand, turn the sword blade edge upward. Split [劈, pi] upwards as the blade moves back and to the left until reaching the level of the upper ribs. Bend the left arm and put the hand on the lower back. The right foot shifts forward diagonally [southwest] half a step.

Shift the weight to the right leg and raise the left foot onto the ball. Turn it to the left and step forward one step at an angle [southwest]. Shift the weight to the left foot; pick up the right foot and put it down in front [of the rear foot]. Raise the left heel. (This is an Empty Stance [meaning, one leg supports the weight and the other leg is insubstantial. Also called a Cat Stance or Insubstantial Stance].)

The sword follows the left foot in the forward stepping gesture as it moves from back to front [east to west]. When moving towards the right [west] in a slanting direction, turn the wrist upwards in a snapping [崩, beng] gesture. Put the left hand on the back of the right wrist. Seat the waist and relax the pelvis. The body moves into a low squatting position. (See Illustration #11.)

Internal Instructions
Retain a light energy on top of the head.
Hollow the chest and raise the back.
Center the body and ensure that it is upright.
Draw in the Tail Gateway.
The spirit of the eyes gazes directly forward.

Application
First, move towards the back [east] and split [劈, pi]. Next, move right [west] at an angle; turn over your right wrist and snap [崩, beng] the opponent's wrist.

9. The Wasp Entering the Hive
黄蜂入洞,
Huang Feng Ru Dong
Face Southeast

Posture Instructions
(Face towards the right diagonal direction.)
Withdraw the left foot one step with the body facing back [south]. Turn the body

towards the left (facing the opposite diagonal direction) [southeast].

Simultaneously, lower the sword tip downward. Move it towards the right and direct it inward (from its original outward position) in a circling motion.

Next, turn over the right wrist so that the sword spine faces upward. The left hand is put under the right hand holding the sword. The waist and legs then make a forward advancing gesture, as the left foot steps forward [southeast]. The left and right hand simultaneously press forward and stab [刺, ci] levelly. (The sword tip faces downward.)

Bend the left knee and gradually straighten the right leg. (See Illustration #12.)

Internal Instructions
Suspend the head so the body is upright.
Draw in the Tail Gateway and relax the waist and pelvis.
The two arms evenly hold the sword and maintain a slight
    bend.
The spirit of the eyes gazes directly forward.

Application
First, stir up [攪, jiao] the opponent's sword or wrist. After turning [southeast], stab [刺, ci] levelly at the opponent's knee.

10. The Spirit of the Cat Catches the Rat
靈貓捕鼠, Ling Mao Bu Shu
Face Southeast

Part One

Posture Instructions
(Face towards the right diagonal direction.) Raise the right leg to the front of the body as if to step forward. Bend the knee. The thigh is parallel with the ground and the foot is pointing down. Bring the right knee back slightly and seat it.

(一) 鼠捕猫靈 (13)

The two hands holding the sword draw it back at chest level. The sword tip points slightly upwards. (See Illustration #13.)

Internal Instructions
Retain a light energy on top of the head.
Hollow the chest and raise the back.
Draw in the Tail Gateway.
Relax the two elbows and suspend them downwards.

Application

From the lower extremities the sword tip is snapped [崩, beng] upwards at the opponent's wrist.

Part Two

[Face Southeast] (The direction is unchanged.) The right foot drops to the ground. Raise the left foot and step forward by jumping and dropping in one step. The right foot returns to the position of Part One (knee up) and then it leaps forward one step. This is the second step with the right foot. The feet finish in a Bow Stance [facing southeast].

(二) 鼠捕貓罢 (14)

Grasp the sword with both hands as the two feet make the forward leaping gesture. (The first right step and then left step.) When the right foot makes its advance-stepping gesture (second step), draw the sword back and move it forward in a counterclockwise circle. As you step forward, stab [刺, ci] levelly at the stomach. (See Illustration #14.)

Internal Instructions

Suspend the head from above so that the body is upright. Sink the shoulders and suspend the elbows downwards.

Hollow the chest and raise the back.
Relax the waist and coccyx.
As both feet drop to the ground, they are first insubstantial and afterward substantial.
Bend the two arms slightly as if holding a ball.
The spirit of the eyes gazes directly forward.

11. The Dragonfly Sipping Water
蜻蜓點水,
Qing Ting Tian Shui
Face Southeast

(二) 鼠捕貓靈 (14)

Posture Instructions
(The direction is unchanged.) Holding the sword with both hands, draw it back to follow the waist and legs as the weight is briefly shifted onto the left leg. The body, however, circles slightly forward first before going backward. Next, continue the waist and leg movement by pressing forward again and moving downward to stab [刺, ci] at knee level. This is just like the inside containment of *The Spirit of the Cat Catches the Rat*, Part Two. (The end position is the same as Illustration #14.)

Internal Instructions
Suspend the head.
Hollow the chest and raise the back.
Gaze forward.

Application
First, move back to neutralize and then return to stab [刺, ci] the opponent's knee.

12. The Swallow Entering the Nest
燕子入巢, Yan Zi Ru Chao

Part One
[Face North]

(一) 巢入子燕 (15)

Posture Instructions
(Face towards the front.) Lean the body to the left and bend the left knee, committing all the weight to the left leg. Gradually straighten the right leg. Simultaneously, carry [带, dai] the sword back and to the left. Place the two fingers, middle and index, of the left hand on the right Pulse Gate. The body shifts into a slight squatting position. (See Illustration #15.)

Internal Instructions

Retain a light and sensitive energy on top of the head.
Sink the shoulders.
Relax the waist and coccyx.
Do not bring the elbows too close to the body.
The spirit of the eyes gazes directly at the sword tip.

Application

When turning to the left, carry [带, dai] to the opponent's hand or wrist.

Part Two

[Face Northeast]
(Face towards the right diagonal direction.) Lean the body to the right. Bend the right knee and commit all the weight to the right leg. Gradually straighten the right leg.

Simultaneously turn over the right wrist, with the sword circling over, so that the palm faces out. As the body shifts to the right, hold the palm levelly. Place the two fingers of the left hand on the back of the right wrist. The body lowers slightly. (See Illustration #16.)

(二) 巢入子燕 (16)

Internal Instructions
The same as Part One.

Application
Levelly draw in the sword to the opponent's wrist or body. This is a waiting gesture [to see the opponent's next move].

Part Three
[Southeast]
(Turn completely around so the direction is unchanged.) Raise the heel of the left foot so that the ball of the foot still adheres to the ground. Pivot the foot to the left. Shift the weight to the left foot and pick up the right foot. In the counterclockwise direction make a full circle, placing the right foot down behind the left. Shift the weight to the right foot; the left foot then steps forward one step. The feet finish in a Bow Stance [facing southeast].

（三）巢入子燕（17）

Simultaneously, the sword follows this gesture by turning leftward levelly while the body circles. It arrives at the time of the forward stab [刺, ci] in a level position [southeast].

Extend the sword forward at stomach level with the palm up. During this time, the left hand separates (from the Pulse Gate), and moves out in front of the forehead. (See Illustration #17.)

Internal Instructions
When circling, clearly distinguish the substantial and
    insubstantial aspect of the feet.
When the center of balance is on the left leg, stab [刺, ci]
    to the front.
Hollow the chest and raise the back.
Seat the waist and relax the coccyx.
Suspend the head so that the body is upright.
Draw in the Tail Gateway.
The spirit of the eyes gazes directly forward.
The left palm faces outward and the arm maintains
    a slight bend.

Application
Circle the body, then stab [刺, ci] the opponent's knee or stomach.

13. Phoenix Spreading Both Wings
鳳凰雙展翅,
Feng Huang Shuang Zhan Chi
Face Northwest

翅 展 雙 凰 鳳 (18)

Posture Instructions
(Turn the body towards the left diagonal direction.) The weight shifts to the right leg and the body turns rightward. As the body turns, pivot the left foot inward. The heel of the left foot remains on the ground.

Shift the weight back to the left leg. The body continues to follow the waist and legs to the right, with the right foot stepping forward one half step [in the northwest direction]. Bend the right knee and seat it firmly. The legs finish in a Bow Stance.

The sword follows the waist and legs during the turning [or revolving] gesture to the right and strikes levelly [in the northwest direction]. The right palm remains upward during the complete movement. The left hand simultaneously moves back, finishing with the palm down. (See Illustration #18.)

Internal Instructions
Retain a light energy on top of the head.
Hold the body upright and draw in the Tail Gateway.
The spirit of the eyes gazes at the sword tip.

Application
When moving and turning rightward, strike to the opponent's ear.

14. Whirlwind to the Right
右旋風,
You Xuan Feng
Face Southwest

翅 展 雙 鳳 凰 (18)

Posture Instructions
(Face towards the left diagonal direction.) Pick up the left foot and step forward one half step (ending in a Substantial Stance [a type of Bow Stance, with 60 percent of the weight in the forward leg]). Shift the weight from the right foot so that it is insubstantial.

    Turn the sword over counterclockwise so the right palm faces down at the front of the chest. Bend the right elbow and hang it downward. With the right hand holding the sword, follow the waist and legs in a forward circling gesture to the front [north], by turning to the right in a clockwise direction. The right foot pivots to the right, on the ball of the foot [to point east]. Transfer the weight to the right foot. Pick up the left foot and place it at the left diagonal [pointing the toes to the southeast]. Both feet are now turned inward.

Next, move downwards to the [west], and around to finish the circle. The sword tip points slightly downward. This posture can be repeated in succession, but preferably not more than three times.

The weight shifts to the left foot and the right foot presses forward at an angle [southwest]. It is first insubstantial, and after advancing forward, substantial. The feet finish in a Bow Stance [pointing southwest].

The left hand moves to the back, levelly and extends outward [in the northeast direction]. The two fingers, middle and index, straighten.

When circling the sword around, it is the waist and legs which move and turn, not the hands and wrists, or upper arms and shoulders. As the sword moves outward [in the southwest direction], the right hand holding the sword turns upward. [Same as Illustration #18, but facing southwest.]

Internal Instructions

When stepping forward, clearly distinguish the substantial
  and insubstantial aspects.
Suspend the head to relax the body and maintain an upright
  position.
Hollow the chest and raise the back.
The spirit of the eyes gazes at the sword tip.

Application
When advancing forward, stir up [攪, jiao] the opponent's hand or wrist.

15. Minor Star of the Dipper
小魁星,
Xiao Kui Xing
Face Southeast

星 魁 小 (19)

Posture Instructions
(Face towards the left diagonal direction.)
To connect this posture with the previous circling posture, turn over the [right] wrist so that the sword follows the waist and legs slightly to the left. The sword circles counterclockwise at an angle to the left side of the body, splitting [劈, pi] downward and to the rear, until it reaches the level of the left rib area.

    The weight remains on the right leg. During the sword movement, the left foot moves forward one step and remains insubstantial. [The stance should be such that the feet are in an Empty Stance with the body facing southeast.]

    The sword continues to move upwards as the [right] wrist turns over. The wrist performs a snapping motion as it turns to finish outward. Place the left two fingers on the back of the right wrist. Maintain the center of balance on the right leg as the body moves down into a slight squatting position. Seat the waist, relax the pelvis, and sink into the legs. (See Illustration #19.)

Internal Instructions
Adhere the qi to the back of the spine.
Center the body and ensure it is upright.
Draw in the Tail Gateway.
The spirit of the eyes gazes directly forward.

Application
When first moving, split [劈, pi] to the rear. Next, when pressing forward, snap [崩, beng] the opponent's wrist [a type of flicking movement].

16. Whirlwind to the Left
左旋風,
Zuo Xuan Feng
Southeast

Posture Instructions
(Withdraw to the rear in the same direction, which does not change.) Withdraw the left foot behind the right foot; seat it firmly.

(二) 蛇尋草掰 (22)

Advance the right foot forward [to the north] one half step (becoming an Empty Stance). [Turn the right foot inward].

Draw the sword back and point it downwards, bringing it around to the front of the chest. Bend the right elbow so it hangs downward.

The waist and legs follow this movement as the sword makes a circling gesture towards the left and up [counter-clockwise, towards the left and returns southeast]. Then, moving down and to the left, make one complete circle. (The sword tip faces slightly down, and it is immaterial how many circles are made.)

Simultaneously the left foot withdraws. First it is insubstantial, then substantial. The right foot follows this movement by first being substantial and then insubstantial. (The number of steps taken is immaterial.)

The left hand as usual moves back and stretches out levelly, with the two fingers, middle and index, straightening.

This posture can be done in succession. However, it should not be performed more than three times. This is just like the inside containment of *Whirlwind to the Right*. [Ending position is similar to Illustration #18, but facing southeast.]

Internal Instructions
Retain a light energy on top of the head.
Hold the body upright and draw in the Tail Gateway.
The spirit of the eyes gazes at the sword tip.

Application
After withdrawing, stir up [搅, jiao] the opponent's hand or wrist.

17. Fishing Posture
等魚式, Deng Yu Shi
Face Northwest

式 魚 等 (20)

Posture Instructions
(Face towards the left diagonal direction.)
To connect this posture with the previous one, *Whirlwind to the Left*, withdraw into a turning gesture to the right. Shift the weight to the right leg. Withdraw the left foot and seat it firmly. The weight shifts back to the left leg.

Raise the sword upwards and press forward [in the northwest direction], striking as it goes out (with the tip of the sword continuing downwards). Simultaneously, the right foot shifts back one half step, with the heel up in an Empty Stance.

The left hand moves back so that the arms are on line. The body moves into a slight squatting position. (See Illustration #20.)

Internal Instructions
Retain a light energy on the top of the head.
Hollow the chest and raise the back.
Sink the shoulders and lower the elbows.
Draw in the Tail Gateway so the body is upright.

Relax the waist and pelvis.
Sink the qi to the Dan Tian.
The spirit of the eyes gazes at the sword tip.

Application
Point [點, dian] to the opponent's hand or wrist.

18. Stir Up the Grass and Search for the Snake
撥草尋蛇, Bo Cao Xin She
Face West

Part One

Posture Instructions
(Face towards the left.) Press forward [west] with the right foot one half step and set the foot down. Bend the knee and seat it firmly.

As the right foot steps, turn the right wrist over so that the back of the hand and the sword blade face upward.

(一) 蛇尋草撥 (21)

As the waist presses forward and downward to the right, move the sword downward and slice levelly at leg height. Gradually straighten the left leg. The legs finish in a Bow

Stance. At the same time, place the left two fingers on the back of the right wrist. (See Illustration #21.)

Internal Instructions
Suspend the head from above so that the body is upright,
Draw in the Tail Gateway.
Do not bend forward.
The sword is held levelly.
Gaze diagonally to the right.

Application
Use a drawing-back intercept [截, jie] to the opponent's leg, stab [刺, ci] the knee, or press [壓, ya] on their sword.

Part Two
[Face West]
(Face towards the left.) Pick up the left foot and step forward one half step. Bend the knee and seat the leg firmly. Simultaneously, turn over the right wrist so that the palm and the sword blade face upward.
     The waist then presses forward and downwards as the legs lower into a squatting position.

(二) 蛇尋單掇 (22)

Moving down, intercept [截, jie] levelly, and then straighten the right leg gradually. The legs finish in a diagonal Bow Stance. At the same time, the left hand moves back and up [to point southeast]. Hold the left arm straight at shoulder level. (See Illustration 22.)

Internal Instructions
The sword should go out levelly, but neither too high
    nor too low.
The eyes gaze levelly.
Suspend the head from above so the body is upright.
Relax the waist and coccyx.

Application
The application is the same as *Stir Up the Grass and Search for the Snake*, Part One, except that this is the left style.

Chen Kung's Comment
When practicing *Stir Up the Grass and Search for the Snake*, you can continue this progression of moving right and left repeatedly; however, you must finish with the [right] Part One style. Therefore, if no additional series of gestures are performed, complete the Part One movements one more time [also ending in the west direction].

19. Embrace the Moon in the Chest
懷中抱月,
Huai Zhong Bao Yue
Face South

(23)

Posture Instructions
(Face towards the rear.) In joining with the previous posture of *Stir Up the Grass and Search for the Snake*, Right Style, draw the left foot back one half step and shift the weight to the left foot. The right foot follows the gesture by also moving back one half step. The right heel is off the ground.

Facing the back [south], draw in as if embracing the sword by the front of the chest. The body moves down into a slight squatting position. Place the left fingers, middle and index, on the right Pulse Gate. (See Illustration #23.)

Internal Instructions
Suspend the head so that the body is upright.
Draw in the Tail Gateway.
Hollow the chest and raise the back.
Sink the qi to the Dan Tian.
Gaze directly forward.

Application
Carry [帶, dai] to the opponent's hand or wrist.

20. Send the Bird Up Into the Trees
送鳥上林,
Song Niao Shang Lin
Face West

林 上 鳥 送 (24)

Posture Instructions
(Face towards the left.) The sword follows the waist and legs into a low squatting posture by turning downward and moving to the front as the weight shifts to the right leg. The body [then] continues in an ascending motion. As this happens, stab [刺, ci] forward and upward until the sword tip rises above the head. (The right palm faces up.)

At the same time, move the left hand back and upward. The left hand extends outward [in the southeast direction] at shoulder level. Raise the left leg, bending the knee. Allow the foot to point down. The center of balance is on the right leg. Lean the upper body slightly to the right [west]. (See Illustration #24.)

Section One: Tai Ji Sword

Internal Instructions
Retain a nimble energy on top of the head.
The substantial and insubstantial must be clearly distinguished.
Gaze upwards.

Application
From a downward position, move up and stab [刺, ci] the knee, stomach, and throat.

21. Black Dragon Wagging Its Tail
烏龍擺尾,
Wu Long Bai Wei
Face West

尾 擺 龍 烏 (25)

Posture Instructions
(Face towards the left.) Place the left foot on the ground behind the right foot and seat it firmly. Transfer the weight to the left leg and raise the right heel so that the foot points towards the ground. This leg is insubstantial [no weight upon it].

The sword follows the waist and legs into a low squatting position. As the waist turns slightly rightward while the body drops, intercept [截, jie] levelly to the right knee. The left hand,

51

at the same time, moves back with the palm facing downward. (See Illustration #25.)

Internal Instructions
Retain a nimble energy on top of the head.
Hollow the chest and raise the back.
Draw in the Tail Gateway.
Gaze at the sword blade.

Application
Intercept [截, jie] to the opponent's wrist, body, or knee.

22. The Wind Rolls Up the Lotus Petals
風捲荷葉, Feng Quan He Ye
Face West

Posture Instructions
[Part One]
(Face towards the left.) Pick up the right foot and place it down in a lateral position so it points diagonally [northwest]. The sword, following the gesture, makes a small, clockwise circle as it turns face up and moves to the left and then returns facing down.

[Illustration #26]

Section One: Tai Ji Sword

Shift the weight to the right leg. Step forward [west] with the left foot; bend the knee and seat it firmly. The legs finish in a Bow Stance [facing west]. Bring the sword to the right side of the body [at waist level] and press forward, stabbing [刺, ci] levelly [palm faces up]. Raise the left hand simultaneously in front of the forehead. (See Illustration #26.)

[Part Two]
Turn over the right wrist. Move the sword leftward. Withdraw it, facing down, in a circular motion, [counterclockwise]. Again, turn to the right and pierce [擊, ji] out. (The tip of the sword faces upwards and the back of the hand is facing upwards.) Place the left-hand two fingers directly on top of the back of the right wrist. The upper body leans slightly towards the right [west]. (See illustration 27.)

(二) 葉荷捲風 (27)

Internal Instructions
Preserve a light energy on the top of the head.
Hold in the chest and raise the back.
Sink the shoulders and suspend the elbows.
Do not stoop forward.
Gaze straight ahead.

Application
Stir up [攪, jiao] the wrist. Stab [刺, ci] the heart or the stomach. When turning over the wrist, pierce [擊, ji] out to the opponent's head.

23. The Lion Shaking Its Head
獅子搖頭, Shi Zi Yao Tou
Face East

Part One

Posture Instructions
(Turn the body towards the right.) Turn the left heel outward. Shift the weight back to the left leg. The right foot then follows the entire body when turning rightward, clockwise, to the front; seat it firmly. The left foot turns in. The legs finish in a diagonal Bow Stance [facing east].

(一) 頭搖子獅 (28)

Simultaneously, the sword follows the body's circular gesture. When turning right, the sword lashes [抽, chou] levelly [this is a drawing-in gesture]. The back of the right hand faces up. Place the two fingers of the left hand, middle and index, on the back of the right wrist. (See Illustration #28.)

Internal Instructions

Clearly discriminate between the substantial and insubstantial aspects of the legs.
Preserve a light energy on the top of the head.
Hold in the chest and straighten the back.
Sink the shoulders and lower the elbows.
Do not stoop forward.
Gaze straight ahead.

Application

When circling the body, lash [抽, chou] the opponent's hand or wrist, or perhaps the trunk area.

Part Two
[Face East]
(Face towards the right.)
Pick up the left foot; move it to the left and put it down on the ground [pointing north]. Bend the left knee and seat it firmly. The right leg then gradually straightens, with the heel of the right foot shifting slightly to the left [turning it in]. The legs finish in a Bow Stance.

(二) 頭搖子獅 (29)

Turn up the right wrist (so the right palm faces upwards). Carry [帶, dai] the sword levelly when turning left. Place the two fingers of the left hand, middle and index, on the right Pulse Gate. (See Illustration #29.)

Application
Towards the left, carry [帶, dai] to the opponent's hand or wrist.

[Transition Move Back to Part One, Right Style]
Next, repeat gesture one, just like *The Lion Shaking Its Head,* Part One.

After completing this form [Part Two, left style], shift the weight to the right foot, and then step back with the left foot one half step and point it straight ahead [east]. The right foot changes to an Empty Step [and withdraws backward]. Shift the weight back into the right leg, turn over the right wrist with the sword following the waist and legs and, pointing it forward [east], lash [抽, chou] out levelly. The legs finish in a diagonal Bow Stance [facing east]. [See Illustration 28.]

Chen Kung's Comment
When practicing *The Lion Shaking Its Head* posture, both styles (Parts One and Two), you may perform the withdraw step repeatedly. How many times it is repeated does not matter. However, you must end with the Part One style.

24. The Tiger Embracing Its Head
虎抱頭,
Hu Bao Tou
Face East

頭　抱　虎 (30)

Posture Instructions
(Face towards the right.) In joining this posture with the previous posture of *The Lion Shaking Its Head*, Part One, the left foot withdraws one half step [to point northeast]. Slightly bend the left knee and end in a Substantial Stance. Next, the right foot shifts back and to the left, one half step. Raise the heel and place the toes directly on the ground and do not commit any weight to the right leg, so to complete an Empty Stance.

Turn up the right wrist (so the palm faces up), with the sword turning towards the left [counterclockwise]; carry [帶, dai] it levelly until it reaches the front of the chest. Then hollow the chest and raise the back. Relax the waist and coccyx as the body moves down into a low squatting gesture. Draw in the sword and arms when moving back; the left hand (palm facing up) holds the back of the right hand from below. Hold the sword with the sword tip pointing slightly up. (See Illustration #30.)

Internal Instructions

Preserve a light energy on the top of the head.
Hold in the chest and straighten the back.
Sink the shoulders and lower the elbows.
Draw in the Tail Gateway.
Gaze straight ahead.

Application

Stir-up [攪, jiao] the opponent's wrist, evading their stab [刺, ci] to your knee. You can also pierce [擊, ji] their wrist or stab [刺, ci] their throat.

25. The Wild Horse Leaps Over the Mountain Stream
野馬跳澗,
Ye Ma
Tiao Jian
Face East

Posture Instructions

(Face towards the right.) Raise the right foot and press forward by jumping to advance one half step. The left foot is then raised upwards. [Set the right foot down and briefly shift the weight to it.] Then leap forward one full step (transferring the weight to the left leg).

Again leap forward with the right foot one full step. Shift the weight forward with the right knee bent (transferring the weight to the right leg).

Simultaneously, with the two hands embracing the sword, first move forward slightly and then draw the sword back in a circular motion [counterclockwise] to the front of the chest. As the right leg advances forward during the second step, stab [刺, ci] levelly. (See Illustration #31.)

Internal Instructions
Preserve a light energy on the top of the head.
Hollow the chest and straighten the back.
Keep the body upright by drawing in the Tail Gateway.
Sink the shoulders and lower the elbows.
The eyes gaze straight ahead.

Application
When leaping forward, stab [刺, ci] the opponent's heart.

26. Turn the Body to Restrain the Horse
翻身勒馬,
Fan Shen Le Ma
Face West

馬 勒 身 翻 （32）

Posture Instructions
(Turn the body towards the left.) Shift the weight to the left leg. Turn in the right foot [to point northwest] and shift the weight to it. Continue to turn the whole body until it faces left [west]. When moving left, draw in [the sword] levelly. Draw the left foot back slightly, with the heel raised.

    The two hands embrace the sword. Depress the chest and straighten the back. When shifting the left foot back, draw in the sword slightly with the sword tip pointing upward. (See Illustration #32.)

Internal Instructions
Clearly discriminate between the substantial and
    insubstantial.
Retain a light energy on top of the head.
Hollow the chest and straighten the back.
Draw in the Tail Gateway to be centered and upright.
Direct the spirit of the eyes to gaze to the front.

Application
Turn the body, carry [帶, dai] and draw into the opponent's wrist, and wait to see their next move.

27. The Compass
指南針,
Zhi Nan Zhen
Face West

針　南　指　(33)

Posture Instructions
(Face towards the left.) Step forward [west] one half step with the left foot. The right foot follows this gesture by pressing forward to a position parallel with the left foot.

The two hands, embracing the sword during the advance stepping gesture, perform a stabbing [刺, ci] motion at chest level. Lower the body into a slight squatting position. (See Illustration #33.)

Internal Instructions
Suspend the head so that the body is upright.
Hollow the chest and straighten the back.

Sink the shoulders and suspend the elbows.
Keep the Tail Gateway centered and upright.
The spirit of the eyes gazes forward.

Application
When stepping forward, stab [刺, ci] the opponent's heart or stir up [搅, jiao] their hand or wrist.

28. Greeting the Wind to Wipe Away the Dust
迎風揮塵, Ying Feng Tan Chen
Face West

Part One (Right Style)

Posture Instructions
(Face towards the left.) Step forward [west] with the right foot one step. Bend the right knee and seat it firmly. Gradually straighten the left leg (changing to an Insubstantial Stance). The legs finish in a diagonal Bow Stance.

(一) 塵揮風迎 (34)

The sword follows the waist and legs when moving to the right. As it moves up, turn over the right wrist (with the back of the hand facing up) and intercept [截, jie] levelly (the sword tip faces upwards). Place the two fingers of the left hand, middle and index, on the back of the wrist. (See Illustration #34.)

Internal Instructions
Do not lean or stoop the body forward too much.
Suspend the head so that the body is upright.
Draw in the Tail Gateway.
The eyes gaze directly at the sword tip.

Application
When moving forward to the right, intercept [截, jie] levelly, or when drawing in, lash [抽, chou] to the opponent's wrist.

Part Two (Left Style)

(Face towards the left.) Step forward [west] with the left foot one-half step, bending the knee and seating it firmly. The right leg then gradually straightens as it (changes into an Insubstantial Stance). The legs end in a diagonal Bow Stance [facing west].

(二) 塵撣風迎 (35)

Turn over the right wrist (so that the palm faces up). The sword, following the waist and legs, moves forward to the left, and intercepts [截, jie] levelly (with the sword tip pointing upward). Place the two fingers of the left hand on the Pulse Gate of the right wrist. (See Illustration #35.)

Internal Instructions
The same as Part One.

Application
When moving towards the left, clear [洗, xi] to the opponent's hand and wrist or their chest.

Chen Kung's Comment
After completing *Greeting the Wind to Wipe Away the Dust*, (Part Two), perform [Part One] again [so that three postures are performed].

29. Drifting With the Current
顺水推舟,
Shun Shui
Tui Zhou
Face West

舟 推 水 顺 (36)

Posture Instructions (Face towards the left.) To join this posture with the previous one, *Greeting the Wind to Wipe Away the Dust,* Part One, turn the sword down and then bring it back up to provoke the opponent, until it reaches the right side of the body.

When turning over the right wrist, simultaneously lift the right foot and step forward [west] one half step and put it down in a cross step. The left foot follows the gesture, pressing forward [west] one full step [so the legs finish in a Bow Stance facing west].

Raise the sword to ear level, as it follows the movement of the waist and legs. As the left foot shifts forward, stab [刺, ci] levelly (with the Tiger's Mouth facing outward). Place the left hand two fingers, middle and index, on the back of the right wrist. (See Illustration #36.)

Internal Instructions
Suspend the head to keep the body upright.
Draw in the Tail Gateway.
Do not stoop the body forward.
The spirit of the eyes gazes forward.

Application
When turning back, stir up [搅, jiao] the opponent's knee or wrist. Moving to the front, stab [刺, ci] the opponent's throat.

30. The Meteor Pursues the Moon
流星趕月,
Liu Xing Gan Yue
Face North

Posture Instructions
The sword follows the waist's rightward turning gesture and makes use of a chopping-like split [劈, pi] in a downward motion until it is level with the shoulders [and the sword points east]. At the same time the left hand moves down to the level of the shoulders and extends outward.

月 趕 星 流 (37)

The legs finish in a Horse Stance as the body moves into a low squatting position. (See Illustration #37.)

Internal Instructions
Retain a light energy on top of the head.
Sink the shoulders and suspend the elbows
Keep the Tail Gateway centered and upright.
Sink the qi to the Dan Tian.

Application
When moving to the right at an angle use a chopping-like split [劈, pi] to the back of the incoming opponent's body.

31. The Skylark Flying Over the Waterfall
天鳥飛瀑,
Tian Niao Fei Bao
Face North

Posture Instructions
(Face towards the front.) Draw the sword slightly inward as it circles back, provoking the opponent. During this motion, step forward one whole step with the left foot. The right foot follow steps so that the two feet end up online with

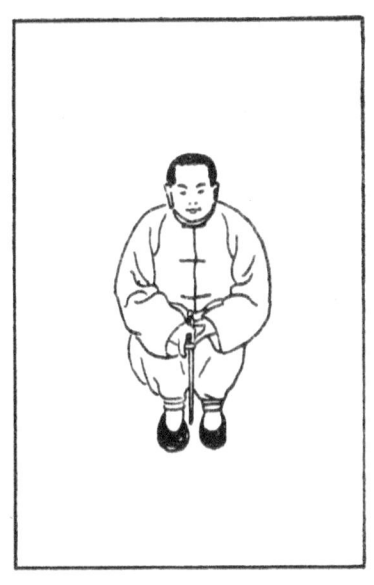

瀑 飛 鳥 天 (38)

each other. Continue to raise the sword back and upwards to ear level; then, turn over the right wrist. This is when the right foot follows with a step forward so that the feet finish parallel to one another. As the right foot steps, press [壓, ya] forward with the sword and cut downward, splitting [劈, pi] to the kneecap [in the north direction].

Place the two fingers of the left hand, middle and index, on the upper side of the right wrist. As the sword completes its cutting motion, bend the knees to lower the body into a squatting position. (See Illustration #38.)

Internal Instructions
Suspend the head so that the body is upright.
Hollow the chest and straighten the back.
Sink the shoulders and suspend the elbows.
Seat the waist and relax the pelvis.
The spirit of the eyes gazes to the front.

Application
When moving to the rear, provoke the opponent by using clearing [洗, xi]. Next, press [壓, ya] to the front and split [劈, pi].

32. Raise the Bamboo Curtain Posture
挑簾式, Tiao Lian Shi
Face Northwest

式 簾 挑 (39)

Posture Instructions
(Face towards the right.) Turn over the right wrist (palm faces up) with the sword turning right and moving upwards. Then circle the sword back towards the left and with a chopping-like split [劈, pi] gesture. Simultaneously, the right foot then steps back half a step [and points toward the northeast].

Raise the left knee so that the thigh is parallel with the ground. The sword follows the rise of the left foot with the right sword-hand rising above the head. The sword tip points down. Place the two fingers of the left hand on the back of the right wrist. (See Illustration #39.)

Internal Instructions
Suspend the head to keep the body upright.
Hollow the chest and raise the back.
Keep the Tail Gateway centered and upright.
The spirit of the eyes gazes forward.

Application

First, turn back and split [劈, pi] to the opponent. Next, turn right to raise [提, ti] the opponent's hand or wrist.

33. Cartwheel Sword, Left and Right
左右車輪劍, Zuo You Che Lun Jian

Posture Instructions
[Part One, Face West]
(Face towards the right.) Place the left foot down in a crosswise step in front of the right foot [pointing north]. Suspend the sword tip at about knee level. Turn to the back [west] and stab [刺, ci] levelly.

Simultaneously bend both knees so the body lowers into a low squatting position. The waist and legs circle towards the left. The eyes follow the sword tip as it moves back [to the west].

Position the left-hand two fingers of the left hand on the back of the right wrist. (See Illustration #40.)

（一）劍輪車右左（40）

Section One: Tai Ji Sword

[Part Two, Face East] Step forward to the right [east] with the right foot one full step. Bend the knees to situate them firmly. The legs end in a Bow Stance. During this movement, direct the sword upward and over, to split [劈, pi] downward to the right (with the palm facing upwards) until it reaches chest level.

(二) 劍輪車右方 (41)

Simultaneously, the left hand opens and separates towards the back, at shoulder level. (See Illustration #41.)

[Part Three, Face West] The waist and legs turn back to the right and the sword follows in a circling movement. Facing to the rear [west], provoke the opponent. The spirit of the eyes gazes directly back at the sword tip. Simultaneously, the left hand opens and

(三) 劍輪車右左 (42)

71

separates, positioned to the front [east] at shoulder level. (See Illustration #42.)

Internal Instructions
Clearly distinguish between the substantial and insubstantial aspects.
Retain a light energy on top of the head.
Hollow the chest and raise the spine.
Keep the Tail Gateway centered and upright.
The spirit of the eyes gazes at the sword tip.

Application
First, move back [west] and stab [刺, ci] the opponent's knee. Secondly, press forward [east] and point [點, dian] to the opponent's wrist. Again, circle the body to the rear and provoke the opponent's hand or wrist.

34. The Swallow Holds Mud in Its Mouth
燕子啣泥, Yan Zi Xian Ni
Face East

瀑飛鳥天 (38)

Posture Instructions
(Face towards the right side.) Pick up the left foot and jump forward to the right side. The right foot then follows by stepping forward, so that it is parallel to the left foot in a narrow Horse Stance. Simultaneously turn over the right wrist (Tiger's Mouth faces upwards). As you move to the front, split [劈, pi] downward to the level of the knee. Bend both knees so that the body is in a low squatting position.

Place the two fingers of the left hand, middle and index, on the upper side of the right wrist. This is similar to the previous posture *The Skylark Flying Over the Waterfall* and makes use of an inside intercept [截, jie]. [Same as Illustration #38, except the body faces east].

Internal Instructions
Suspend the head so that the body is upright.
Hollow the chest and raise the back.
Sink the shoulders and suspend the elbows.
Seat the waist and relax the coccyx.
The spirit of the eyes gazes forward.

Application
Step forward to press [壓, ya] and split [劈, pi].

35. The Great Roc Spreading Its Wings
大鵬展翅,
Da Peng Zhan Chi
Face West

Posture Instructions
(Face towards the left side.) Raise the body and then stepping with the right foot, turn the entire body to the right, moving [the right foot] back towards the right side and stepping out one whole step. Bend the right knee and gradually straighten the left leg. The legs finish in a Bow Stance [facing west].

翅 展 鵬 大 (43)

During the rightward turning gesture, follow with the sword by circling it down then upward so that it pierces [擊, ji] levelly (with the palm facing upward). Place the two fingers of the left hand by the crook of the right elbow. (See Illustration #43.)

Internal Instructions
Suspend the head so that the body is upright.
Hollow the chest and raise the back.
Draw in the Tail Gateway.
Do not bend forward or straighten the arms too much.
Gaze directly at the sword tip.

Application
When circling the body, pierce [擊, ji] the opponent's ear gate.

36. Dragging the Moon From the Sea Bottom
海底撈月,
Hai Di Lao Yue
Face East

月　撈　底　海 (44)

Posture Instructions
(Face towards the right.) Shift the left foot slightly to the left [east] by pivoting it on the heel. Transfer the center of gravity (weight) to the left leg. Jump forward one step with the right foot to the front [east]. Bend the knee and seat it firmly. The legs finish in a Bow Stance.

Simultaneously, the sword follows this gesture by circling down and pressing straight forward to provoke the opponent at chest level (with the palm facing upward). At the same time the left hand raises up and moves back, opens, and separates on line with the shoulder. (See Illustration #44.)

Internal Instructions
Do not lean the body forward too much.
The right knee should not pass beyond the tip of the foot.
Retain a light energy on top of the head.
Hollow the chest and raise the back.
Draw in the Tail Gateway.
The spirit of the eyes gazes forward.

Application
When turning the body, carry [帶, dai] to the opponent's knee or wrist, or clear [洗, xi] to their head.

37. Embrace the Moon in the Chest
懷中抱月,
Huai Zhong Bao Yue
Face North

月 抱 中 懷 (45)

Posture Instructions
(Face towards the front.) Draw back the right foot one half step and raise the heel and touch the toes to the ground. Simultaneously bend the knees so that the body is in a squatting position.

[During this motion] draw back the sword to use a drawing in lash [抽, chou] at chest level. Place the two fingers of the left hand, middle and index, on the upper right Pulse Gate. (See Illustration #45.)

Internal Instructions
Suspend the head so that the body is held upright.
Hollow the chest and raise the back.
Sink the shoulders and suspend the elbows.
Draw in the Tail Gateway.
Clearly discriminate between the substantial and the insubstantial aspects.
The spirit of the eyes gazes at the sword tip.

Application
When moving back use a drawing-in lash [抽, chou] at the opponent's hand or wrist.

38. Yaksha Searches the Sea
夜叉探海,
Ye Cha Tan Hai
Face North

海 探 叉 夜 (46)

Posture Instructions
(Face towards the front.) Place down the right foot towards the front with all the weight on the right leg. The left foot, following this movement, is raised up. At the same time, press the sword forward and down in a stabbing [刺, ci] motion. (Tiger's Mouth faces up.) As the sword tip moves down, direct the left hand back. The left arm moves up such that it is on line with the shoulder. The upper body moves into a slightly leaning position. (See Illustration #46.)

Internal Instructions
Suspend the head from above so that the body is upright. Draw in the Tail Gateway.

Section One: Tai Ji Sword

Clearly distinguish the substantial and insubstantial aspects. Gaze directly at the sword tip.

Application
Stab [刺, ci] the opponent's knee.

39. Rhinoceros Gazing at the Moon
犀牛望月,
Xi Niu Wang Yue
Face North

Posture Instructions
(Face towards the front.) Step down with the left foot to the left side [west] at an angle [northwest]. Bend the knee; shift the weight to it and seat it firmly.

月 望 牛 犀 (47)

Gradually straighten the right leg. The legs finish in a Bow Stance.

The sword follows the waist and the legs in a leftward circling gesture. Towards the left [west] move straight back, (with the sword edge facing up) to carry [帶, dai]. Place the middle and index fingers of the left hand on the right Pulse

Gate. The body faces and leans slightly to the left. (See Illustration #47.)

Internal Instructions
Retain a light energy on top of the head.
Hollow the chest and raise the back.
Keep the body upright and draw in the Tail Gateway.
Gaze directly at the sword tip.

Application
When moving left and back, levelly carry [帶, dai] to the opponent's hand or wrist.

40. Shoot the Wild Goose Posture
射雁式,
She Yan Shi
Face Northwest

式 雁 射 (48)

Posture Instructions
(Face towards the left side.) Jump-step to the right side with the right foot one half step [so that the toes point north]. Move the sword upward at an angle to the left, then draw the sword down with a chopping-like motion to split [劈, pi].

The two fingers of the left hand circle to the left and then press outward. The body drops down into a low squatting position.

Continue to draw in the sword until it is in line with the right leg, pointing downward. At the same time, shift the left foot forward slightly; raise the left heel so that the toes point towards the ground. The right leg remains substantial with the left insubstantial. (See Illustration #48.)

Internal Instructions
Suspend the head from above so the body is upright.
Hollow the chest and raise the back.

Sink the shoulders and suspend the elbows.
Draw in the Tail Gateway.
The spirit of the eyes gazes forward.

Application
Split [劈, pi] to the opponent's sword then draw in on the wrist. The two fingers of the left hand are used to strike [點, dian] a pulse or entice [引, yin] the opponent.

41. Green Dragon Stretches Its Claws
青龍採爪,
Qing Long Cai Zhua
Face Northwest

爪 採 龍 青 (49)

Posture Instructions
(Face towards the left side.) Step forward with the left foot one half step [northwest]. The right foot follows this gesture by stepping forward, keeping the heel up, and so that the two feet are parallel. Bend both knees to move the body into a slight squatting position.

    At the same time, the sword follows the forward stepping and squatting motion by moving to the front and stabbing

[刺, ci] levelly (palm faces up). Place the left two fingers on the inner part of the right elbow. (See Illustration #49.)

Internal Instructions
Suspend the head from above so that the body is erect.
Hollow the chest and raise the back.
Draw in the Tail Gateway.
Do not straighten the right arm too much.
Sink the shoulders, lower the elbows, and seat the wrist.
The spirit of the eyes gazes forward.

Application
Stab [刺, ci] the opponent's throat.

42. Phoenix Spreading Both Wings
鳳凰雙展翅,
Feng Huang Shuang Zhan Chi
Face Southeast

翅 展 雙 凰 鳳 (50)

Posture Instructions
(Face towards the right side.)
Raise the right foot, moving it one whole step toward the rear right side. Bend the [right] knee and seat it firmly. The left leg

gradually straightens. Both legs end in a Bow Stance [southeast].

At the same time, the sword follows the body rightward. Turn the sword to the right and upwards, piercing [擊, ji] to the front [southeast] (with the palm facing up). The left hand simultaneously moves back, openly separating. (See Illustration #50.)

Internal Instructions
Do not stoop forward too much.
Do not straighten the right arm too much or hold it too high.
Suspend the head from above so that the body is erect.
Hollow the chest and raise the back.
Draw in the Tail Gateway.
The spirit of the eyes gazes at the sword tip.

Application
Turn the body and pierce [擊, ji] the opponent's ear, or snap [崩, beng] their wrist, but restrain from the intention of stabbing [刺, ci].

43. Crossing and Obstructing, Left and Right
左右跨攔, Zuo You Gua Lan
Face East

Posture Instructions [Part One, Left Style] (Face towards the right.) Pick up the left foot and step forward to the left at an angle [northeast]. Bend the left knee and seat it firmly. Drag the right foot forward to follow this gesture. The right leg ends in an insubstantial position. The legs finish in a Bow Stance.

(一) 攔跨右左 (51)

The sword follows the waist and legs in a leftward leaning gesture. Carry [帶, dai] the sword crosswise to the left [parallel with the ground], with the sword edge facing up and the palm facing inside [towards you].

Place the sword fingers, middle and index, of the left hand on the right Pulse Gate. This is called *Crossing and Obstructing*, Left Style. (See Illustration #51.)

[Part Two, Right Style]
Pick up the right foot and step forward one step to the right side [southeast]. Bend the right knee and seat it firmly. Drag the left foot forward to follow this gesture. The left leg remains insubstantial. The legs end in a Bow Stance.

The sword follows the waist and legs in a rightward leaning gesture. Turn over the right wrist so that the palm faces outward and the sword lashes [抽, chou] crosswise to the right [holding the sword parallel with the ground]. Place the sword fingers of the left hand on the back, upper part of the right wrist. This is called *Crossing and Obstructing, Right Style*. (See Illustration #52.)

（二）攔跨右左（52）

Internal Instructions
Clearly distinguish the insubstantial from the substantial.
Suspend the head so that the body is upright.
Hollow the chest and raise the back.
Relax the waist and pelvis; draw in the Tail Gateway.
The spirit of the eyes gazes at the sword edge.

Application
To the left, carry [帶, dai] to the opponent's wrist. Moving right, lash [抽, chou] to the opponent's wrist.

44. Shoot the Wild Goose Posture
射雁式,
She Yan Shi
Face Southeast

式 雁 射 (48)

Posture Instructions
(Face towards the right side.) Direct the sword upward slightly and to the right with a chopping-like motion and split [劈, pi]. Then withdraw the sword until it is on line with the right leg. During this sword movement pick up the left foot and step forward in front of the right foot; set it down [pointing southeast] with the heel raised and the toes touching the ground, so to complete an Empty Stance. [Same as Illustration #48, but the direction for this posture is southeast.]

Internal Instructions
Suspend the head from above, so that the body is erect.
Hollow the chest and raise the back.
Sink the shoulders and lower the elbows.

Draw in the Tail Gateway.
The spirit of the eyes gazes forward.

Application
Split [劈, pi] to the opponent's sword then draw in on the wrist. The two fingers of the left hand are used to strike [點, dian] a pulse or entice [引, yin] the opponent.

45. White Ape Offering Fruit
白猿獻菓,
Bai Yuan Xian Guo
Face East

Posture Instructions
(Face towards the right.) Step forward to the left with the left foot one half step. The right foot follows this gesture by stepping forward and leftward, with the heel touching first, so that both feet finish in a parallel position.

The sword follows this movement to the left by first moving it back and to the right (palm facing up). Continue to circle the sword to the left, returning it so it is level and ends in front of the body [pointing east].

Simultaneously, the left sword fingers circle back and to the left. As the left hand returns in front of the chest, it embraces the sword (by placing it under the right hand). [As the hands come together], bend the knees to lower the body into a squatting position. (See Illustration #53.)

Application
Stir up [揽, jiao] the opponent's wrist, then stab [刺, ci] their throat.

46. Falling Flowers Posture
落花式, Luo Hua Shi
Face East

Posture Instructions
[Part One, Left Style]
(Face towards the right as the body moves backwards.) Draw the right foot back and to the right [pointing it southeast] one step. The sword follows the waist and legs by first circling to the left and then turning rightward in a withdrawing gesture. As it returns rightward move it upward and turn over the right wrist (so that the palm faces towards the right and

(一) 頭揥子獅 (28)

the blade edge is facing upward). Place the left sword fingers on the back, upper part of the right wrist. This is like the posture *The Lion Shaking Its Head,* Part One style, except the wrist is turned rightward. Only when raising [提, ti] and blocking [格, ge] is the sword held higher. The right foot is behind the left foot. (This is called the left style.) [Similar to Illustration #28.]

[Part Two, Right Style]
Draw the left foot towards the rear and move it leftward at an angle [so that it points northeast]. The sword follows the waist and legs by turning left and back in a withdrawing gesture. To do this, turn over the right wrist so the palm faces up. The sword moves downward at knee level to carry [帶, dai] and block [格, ge]. The left hand follows the gesture but separates and moves to the rear [to point northwest].

The legs [the left foot behind the right foot] finish in a Bow Stance. This is called the right style.

Repeat and withdraw the right foot, with the sword turning up and to the right, raise [提, ti] and block [格, ge]. After finishing the left style, repeat the right style. Perform both the left and right styles twice. It does not matter how many times you step backward as long as you finish with the right style. The movements of the sword must comply with and follow the waist and legs when withdrawing. The sword should fluctuate in an up-and-down gesture, from high, to central, to low, like snowflakes falling down.

Section One: Tai Ji Sword

Internal Instructions

Clearly discriminate between the substantial and the insubstantial.
Suspend the head so the body is erect.
Hollow the chest and raise the back.
Center the posterior to ensure it is upright.
Gaze directly at the sword tip when going up, down, to the left, and to the right.

Application

Up and down, to the left and right, raise [提, ti], block [格, ge], carry [帶, dai], and lash [抽, chou] to the opponent's chest, stomach, wrist, knee, and leg.

47. Fair Lady Weaving at the Shuttles
玉女穿梭,
Yu Nu Chuan Suo
Face North

披穿女玉 (54)

Posture Instructions
(Face towards the front.) Join this with the previous posture, *Falling Flowers,* Right Style.

　　Turn over the right wrist (so that the palm faces up). Direct the sword tip behind, towards the left [west] in a circular motion. Return the sword to the front, turning it down and slightly to the right so that the sword tip is held low and stabs [刺, ci] downwards (so the palms face upwards and the sword tip points down). Simultaneously, the body turns leftward with the left foot stepping forward one half step [north]. Bend the knee and seat it firmly. The legs finish in a Bow Stance [facing north]. The two hands hold the sword (with the left hand outside of the right hand). (See Illustration #54.)

Internal Instructions
Retain a light energy on top of the head.
Hollow the chest and raise the back.
Keep the Tail Gateway centered and upright.
The spirit of the eyes gazes directly to the front.

Application
First, stir up [攪, jiao] the opponent's wrist, then stab [刺, ci] their stomach or knee.

48. White Tiger Twists Its Tail
白虎攪尾,
Bai Hu Jiao Wei
Face East

尾攪虎白 (55)

Posture Instructions
(Face towards the right.) The sword follows the waist and legs in a rightward turning gesture. Moving towards the right, it moves up in a snapping [崩, beng] motion. The legs first are positioned in a Bow Stance, but afterwards end in a Horse Stance, with the sword tip pointing up. The left hand simultaneously moves to the left side, openly separating [at shoulder height]. The eyes gaze to the right side [east]. (See Illustration #55.) [The direction of the posture is east, but the body is facing north in the Horse Stance.]

Internal Instructions
Retain a light energy on top of the head.
Hollow the chest and raise the back.
Keep the Tail Gateway centered and upright.
Relax the waist and coccyx.
Gaze directly at the sword tip.

Application
Snap [崩, beng] and then pierce [擊, ji] to the opponent's wrist.

49. Carp Leaping Over the Dragon Gate
魚跳龍門,
Yu Tiao Long Men
Face East

[#30]

Posture Instructions
(Face towards the right.) Direct the sword towards the left, drawing it in until it is at the front of the chest, with both hands embracing it. Shift the weight to the left leg and draw the right foot back one half step towards the left foot. Raise the right heel so that the toes point towards the ground. This completes an Empty Stance.

[#31]

[In the next movement] the left leg is slightly bent, finishing in a Substantial Stance. This posture is like *The Tiger Embracing Its Head* [top illustration, #30]. The last part of the movement is like the posture *The Wild Horse Leaps Over the Mountain Stream* [bottom illustration, #31].

Application
See the previous postures of *The Tiger Embracing Its Head* and *The Wild Horse Leaps Over the Mountain Stream* for the applications.

50. Black Dragon Twisting Around a Pillar
烏龍絞柱, Wu Long Jiao Zhu

Posture Instructions
[Part One, Face East]
The sword follows the waist and legs by moving back and towards the left [northeast] in a circling gesture. Turn the [sword] upwards and to the left and then with an upwards chopping-like movement, split [劈, pi] towards the back and online with the left rib area. The left hand follows this gesture by openly separating towards the back.

(一) 烏龍絞柱 (56)

    The left foot steps forward [east], one half step. Raise the heel and touch the toes to the ground, this completes an Empty Stance [no weight on the left leg].

    Simultaneously, the sword follows the waist and legs by pressing forward in a circling gesture. Moving low, facing the front, turn over the sword with a snapping [崩, beng] motion. As it moves up, perform raising [提, ti]. Place the left sword fingers on the upper back area of the right wrist. (See Illustration #56.)

[Part Two,
Face Southwest]
The body is turned towards the back with the left foot slightly straightened, completing an Insubstantial Stance. Bend the right knee, placing all the weight on the right leg. The legs finish in a Bow Stance.

(二) 柱絞龍烏 (57)

The sword, following this gesture, moves up, to the right, and back as it splits [劈, pi]. Simultaneously, the left hand [and arm] opens and separates online with the shoulders towards the front [east]. (See Illustration #57.)

[Part Three, Face East]
Turn the left foot out [northeast] and shift the weight to it. Pick up the right foot and step out towards the front [east] Bend the right knee and seat it firmly, and gradually straighten the left leg. (The legs finish in a Bow Stance.)

(三) 柱絞龍烏 (58)

At the same time, the sword follows the waist and legs in moving forward to the front [east]. Moving low, stab [刺, ci] with the sword straight forward (the palm faces up). This is like the posture *Drag the Moon From the Sea Bottom*, only here the sword stabs [刺, ci] outward at the right armpit level.

Raise the left hand upward so that it is in front of the forehead with the palm facing out, straightening the index and middle fingers. (See Illustration #58.)

Internal Instructions
Clearly distinguish the substantial and insubstantial aspects.
The sword, waist, and legs move in unison.
Suspend the head so the body is upright.
Hollow the chest and raise the back.
Keep the Tail Gateway centered and upright.
The spirit of the eyes gazes directly forward.

Application
Shifting back [northwest], perform a splitting [劈, pi] motion and going forward [east] perform a snapping [崩, beng] (also raising [提, ti]) gesture. When returning back [southwest], perform a splitting [劈, pi] motion and when pressing forward [east], carry [帶, dai] and stab [刺, ci] to the opponent's heart.

51. Immortal Guiding the Way
仙人指路, Xian Ren Zhi Lu
Face North

Posture Instructions
[Part One]
(Face towards the front.) Withdraw the left foot slightly one half step. Bend the [left] knee and seat it firmly. Gradually straighten the right leg. The legs end in a Bow Stance.

The sword follows the waist and legs by moving towards the left and back in a turning gesture.

In going back, draw the sword inward at nose level with the palm facing inwards. The sword blade edge faces up.

Place the left hand sword fingers on the right Pulse Gate, with the eyes gazing at the sword tip. (See Illustration #59.)

（一）路指人仙（59）

[Part Two]
Next, turn towards the right, bending the right leg and seating it firmly. The left leg gradually straightens so that the legs are again in a Bow Stance.

Simultaneously, turn over the right wrist so that the palm faces out. Carry [帶, dai] and draw in as the sword moves rightward. Place the left-hand sword fingers on the back upper part of the right wrist. Gaze directly at the sword tip. (See Illustration #60.)

(二) 路指人仙 (60)

Internal Instructions
Retain a light energy on top of the head.
Hollow the chest and straighten the back.
Keep the body erect by drawing in the Tail Gateway.
Relax the waist and coccyx.
The spirit of the eyes gazes directly to the front.

Application
To the left and right sides, carry [帶, dai] and block [格, ge] the opponent's wrist.

52. The Wind Sweeps Away the Plum Blossoms
風掃梅花, Feng Sao Mei Hua
Face North

Posture Instructions
(Completely circle around to face towards the front.) Raise the right heel. The sword blade faces out with the palm facing downward. Raise the left foot. Turn the whole body towards the right on the ball of the right foot, completing one big circle [in a clockwise direction]. At the same time the sword follows the left foot in the circling gesture, turning right and sweeping levelly throughout the entire large circling gesture. Stop when reaching the original position [north]. Put the left foot down close to its original position. The position of the sword is unchanged.

When turning, clearly discriminate the substantial and insubstantial aspects. Gaze directly at the sword tip. Do not be hurried [with the circling gesture] or go too slowly; it is essential that the sword, waist, and legs move in unison. (No Illustration.)

Application
The sword sweeps and carries [帶, dai] completely around at the coming opponent.

53. Holding Up the Ivory Tablet
手捧牙笏,
Shou Peng Ya Hu
Face North

笏牙捧手 (61)

Posture Instructions
(Face towards the front.) Bring the sword tip down low, turning it right and back. Return it to the front by completely circling it in one [clockwise] motion. Pick up the left foot and step forward [north] one step. The right foot follows this gesture with the heel landing first so that the tips of the feet are in line. This is the same as the *Beginning Posture*. (With the shoulders held levelly.) Bend the knees to lower the body into a low squatting position. Both hands embrace the sword as it moves forward and upward, stabbing [刺, ci] levelly. The sword tip faces upwards. (See Illustration #61.)

Internal Instructions
Retain a light energy on top of the head.
Hollow the chest and raise the back.
Sink the shoulders and suspend the elbows.
Draw in the Tail Gateway.
Relax the waist and coccyx.
The spirit of the eyes gazes directly forward.

Application
First, stir up [攪, jiao] the opponent's sword, then step up and stab [刺, ci] their heart or throat.

54. Embrace the Sword and Return to the Origin
抱劍歸原,
Bao Jian Gui Yuan
Face North

(一) 抱劍歸原 (62)

Posture Instructions
The body ascends slightly, with the right thumb supporting the sword. The left palm joins with it. (See Illustration #62.)

[Transfer the sword to the left hand]. As the body rises upwards, turn over the right wrist. The sword tip faces forward and is lowered with the sword blade facing up. The left hand holding the sword turns it down and back so that the sword is next to the left arm, which turns outwards. Simultaneously, raise the right hand up to the chest level and then down in a pressing and sinking motion. This is the same as the *Beginning Posture*. (See Illustration #63.)

(二) 抱劍歸原 (63)

(Returning to the Origin, it is desirable to study this type of drawing in type of movement so to end in the same stance as with the *Beginning Posture*. The sword movement is comparable to the withdrawing movement in the *Falling Flowers Posture*.)

Internal Instructions
Suspend the head so the body is erect.
Hollow the chest and straighten the back.
Relax the whole body and return the qi to the Dan Tian.
Gather the qi and solidify the spirit.
Stand idle for a few moments, allowing the qi and blood
    in the whole body to circulate.
Rest with the appearance of Returning to the Origin.[5]

Translator's Note
5. *Returning to the Origin* refers to the Daoist ideal of "Returning to the Dao," "Origin, or "Source." Here, however, the meaning is also to return to the original position from which the sword form began.

Tai Ji Sword Form Postures

1. Beginning Posture 14
2. Step Forward and Unite the Sword Posture 16
3. The Immortal Guiding the Road 17
4. Triple Bracelets Encircling the Moon 19
5. Major Star of the Dipper 22
6. The Swallow Searches for Water 24
7. Obstruct and Sweep, Right and Left 26
8. Minor Star of the Dipper 29
9. The Wasp Entering the Hive 30
10. The Spirit of the Cat Catches the Rat 32
11. The Dragonfly Sipping Water 34
12. The Swallow Entering the Nest 35
13. Phoenix Spreading Both Wings 39
14. Whirlwind to the Right 40
15. Minor Star of the Dipper 42
16. Whirlwind to the Left 43
17. Fishing Posture 45
18. Stir Up the Grass and Search for the Snake 46
19. Embrace the Moon in the Chest 49
20. Send the Bird Up Into the Trees 50
21. Black Dragon Wagging Its Tail 51
22. The Wind Rolls Up the Lotus Petals 52
23. The Lion Shaking Its Head 54
24. The Tiger Embracing Its Head 57
25. The Wild Horse Leaps Over the Mountain Stream 58
26. Turn the Body to Restrain the Horse 60
27. The Compass 61
28. Greeting the Wind to Wipe Away the Dust 62

29. Drifting With the Current 65
30. The Meteor Pursues the Moon 66
31. The Skylark Flying Over the Waterfall 67
32. Raise the Bamboo Curtain Posture 69
33. Cartwheel Sword, Left and Right 70
34. The Swallow Holds Mud In Its Mouth 73
35. The Great Roc Spreading Its Wings 74
36. Dragging the Moon From the Sea Bottom 75
37. Embrace the Moon in the Chest 77
38. Yaksha Searches the Sea 78
39. Rhinoceros Gazing at the Moon 79
40. Shoot the Wild Goose Posture 81
41. Green Dragon Stretches Its Claws 82
42. Phoenix Spreading Both Wings 83
43. Crossing and Obstructing, Left and Right 85
44. Shoot the Wild Goose Posture 87
45. White Ape Offering Fruit 88
46. Falling Flowers Posture 89
47. Fair Lady Weaving at the Shuttles 91
48. White Tiger Twists Its Tail 93
49. Carp Leaping Over the Dragon Gate 94
50. Black Dragon Twisting Around a Pillar 95
51. Immortal Guiding the Way 98
52. The Wind Sweeps Away the Plum Blossoms 100
53. Holding Up the Ivory Tablet 101
54. Embrace the Sword and Return to the Origin 102

Section Two
Tai Ji Saber

太極刀

Chen Kung's Introduction

Tai Ji Saber, also known as Thirteen Posture Saber, has thirteen secret characters [meanings]:[1]

1. Kan 砍 (Chopping)
2. Duo 剁 (Cutting)
3. Chan 剗 (Slicing)
4. Jie 截 (Intercepting)
5. Gua 刮 (Parrying)
6. Liao 撩 (Stirring-Up)
7. Zha 扎 (Piercing)
8. Lu 招 (Clawing)[2]
9. Pi 劈 (Splitting)
10. Chan 纏 (Binding)
11. Shan 搧 (Fanning)
12. Lan 攔 (Obstructing)
13. Hua 滑 (Slipping Upwards)

In former days the Yang family members were the first to arrange the proper names for this weapon within the art of Taijiquan. There are few saber gestures, yet with each gesture you can apply a staggering number of practical applications. Practitioners are unable to fathom them all, since they are vast in number.

At the time when Yang Jianhou transmitted these gestures and wrote the mystical names for saber [which were originally authored by his father Yang Luchan]. Yang [Chengfu] then consented to hand them over to me personally.

Yang [Chengfu] would barely finish wiping the dust from his saber and his advanced level would be obvious, even before taking the first stance. The tip of his saber became the object of his tenaciousness; with nothing more than a simple motion of striking out with his hand, one could observe the wonderfulness and subtlety of the Yang family Tai Ji Saber.

Unfortunately, those able to really acquire the proper transmission of the Tai Ji Saber are few. It's as if this art were lost or hidden, completely separated from the training of Taijiquan. The original authors of these valuable teachings were unwilling to hand them down to others, especially the matters concerning saber practice and practical applications.

Here are some additional details for your examination and reflection:

When either practicing the solo form or the practical applications, the waist and legs should act as the axis or pivot point for every movement.

When advancing or retreating, the saber must move in conjunction with the waist and legs, with each mutually following one another. The saber must be used as if it were just like the empty-hand style.

The entire body must be one unit, whether moving up or down, forward or backward, looking left or gazing right. In the midst of these movements there cannot be the slightest interruption or lack of continuous movement.

If you do not adhere to these principles, the intrinsic energy will not be conveyed into the saber. It will be just brute force. (The energy of idiots!) To fail to adhere to the aforementioned principles results in the intrinsic energy being obstructed internally by your bones, and you will be unable to stimulate it externally. Consequently, there will be corruption in your practice and an unresponsive mobilization of intrinsic energy.

The intrinsic energy must be drawn out from within yourself and into the saber. When using the body and saber as one unit, the intrinsic energy, along with the energies of jin, qi, and shen, will be transmitted to the tip of the saber. This is just like mercury filling the inside of a tube. In practical use it is gathered at the rear of the saber and penetrates to the tip.

The first generation of the Yang family trained with the Tai Ji Saber. The blade itself weighed five catties [5½ pounds], and the point of the saber was able to be twisted and moved about easily so as to draw out the intrinsic energy from its source within the body. In the event that a person uses a really heavy saber, so heavy that they can hardly handle it in the hands [like many kung fu weapons], they would not be able to use the waist and legs properly and, if challenged, would not be quick and spirited.

Therefore, in learning and practicing the Tai Ji Saber, it is false to think that you cannot develop the intrinsic energy and apply the waist and legs to each movement. Regarding Sticking [沾, Zhan], Adhering [黏, Nian], and other intrinsic energies, and in comparison to the empty-hand quan, the methods are the same with Tai Ji Saber. If not, then you could not successfully perform the orthodox teachings of Taijiquan inherent within Tai Ji Saber.

Translator's Note

1. The meanings and uses of the thirteen secret characters are presented within the instructions of the saber postures themselves. The applications of these thirteen characters within saber are quite varied, just as are the Thirteen Posture secret meanings of Taijiquan.

   These applications run from coarse applications to the very subtle, and are correlated with the Thirteen Postures of Taijiquan (see list below). As in the solo form of Taijiquan, the Five Operations (correlations of the Five Elements) of Advancing, Withdrawing, Look-Left, Gaze-Right, and Central Equilibrium are aspects of how the Eight Postures (or operations) function. So Warding-Off (or Chopping) can function with any of the Five Operations, and this is true for the other seven postures and corresponding saber characters. Meaning, the postures and characters of one through eight in the following list can function within the operations and meanings of nine through thirteen. So, as in sword, it is no simple matter of describing the thirteen secret characters as purely individual techniques.

   1. Warding-Off relates with Chopping.
   2. Rolling-Back with Cutting.
   3. Pressing with Slicing.
   4. Pushing with Intercepting.
   5. Pulling with Parrying.
   6. Splitting with Stirring Up.
   7. Elbowing with Piercing.
   8. Shouldering with Clawing.
   9. Advancing with Splitting.

10. Withdrawing with Binding.
11. Looking-Left with Fanning.
12. Gazing-Right with Obstructing.
13. Central Equilibrium with Slipping Upwards.

In looking at the correlations, you can deduce that Chopping, for example, can function in the operations of either Splitting, Binding, Fanning, Obstructing, and Splitting Upwards (as these equate with the Five Operations of body movements).

2. As with the character of Rolling-Back (also pronounced "Lu"), the ideogram for "Clawing" (捛, Lu) is an invented character by the Yang Family, not found in dictionaries.

Tai Ji Saber Praise

*In Seven Star Crouching Tiger, exhibit the mind-intent and qi.*³

When low with the toes of the front foot raised, show great mind-intent and qi to cause the opponent's defeat.

In White Crane Spreading Its Wings, a secret kick is concealed.

The front leg on its toes is a potential kick, which the opponent cannot detect because their upper body is thrown into disorder.

In Wind Sweeps Away Plum Blossoms, a petal is hidden beneath.

After sweeping away the opponent's front leg, yet another sweep comes to the back of their remaining upright leg.

In Pushing Open the Shutters to Gaze at the Moon, the body stretches long.

Long energy is used like leaning out the window to look up at the moon after the shutters have been opened.

In Turn Around to Face Left and Turning to Gaze Right, the bow is drawn to both sides.

In Rolling-Back, the movements resemble an archer drawing back a bow to shoot an arrow.

The Jade Maiden Weaving at Shuttles corresponds to the Eight Directions.

These movements circle about through all the positions of the Eight Diagrams (八卦, Ba Gua).

In Lion Rolling a Ball, roll over to the front.
   The opponent thinks you've fallen, but you rise again like a ball popping up from the water.

Mt. Tai Being Subjected to a Python, turning its body about actively.
   Like a huge snake wrapping itself around a mountain, an opponent cannot find escape.

Right and left, high and low, persistently attach like a Butterfly to the Blossoms.
   No matter where an opponent seeks to move, stick and adhere like a butterfly upon a flower.

Turning the body to Claw and Stir Up is just like a windmill.
   As soon as the opponent feels escape from a claw (捋, lu), the stir up (撩, liao) arrives. As soon as the stir up is completed the claw appears.

With a Double Kick follows a Strike Tiger Posture.
   With the opponent recovering from two kicks, the upper body is vulnerable—a situation in which a Tiger would take advantage.

A Mandarin Duck Stands On One Leg with body aslant.
   It appears to be asleep, appears lost, but the duck is only waiting to fly away diagonally.

Drifting With the Current, the boat pole is lashed out.
   The opponent is taken in and defeated by the lashing of the waves coming at them.

Turn over the body and separate hands to Leap Over the Dragon Gate.
   Like a carp leaping from the water, turn the body and unfold the arms, then the jump can be effective.

Splitting Open Mt. Hua to Embrace the Saber Posture.
After performing split (劈, pi), a returning movement must occur or the mountain will fall upon you.

A Phoenix Carrying a Rock Back to Its Nest takes the Six Harmonies.
The harmony of lightness and nimbleness, the harmony of intrinsic energy (jin) and vital energy (qi), and the harmony of vital energy and spirit (shen) energy.

Translator's Commentary

3. The *Saber Praise* is written in sixteen verses, with seven ideograms in each verse. This "praise" (歌, ge, sometimes translated as "verses" or "song") is a poetic list of names and uses of postures not only in older saber forms, but also in many kung fu styles. Chen Kung simply attached this praise to the beginning of the Taiji Saber form, but offered no explanation or comment on it. This is understandable, because to do so would require a great deal of lengthy citation work to clarify the praise in its entirety. To help shed some light on the verses, I have included the brief statements under each verse.

Tai Ji Saber Form Instructions

1. Beginning Posture
起勢, Qi Shi
Face North

Posture Instructions
The left hand holds the saber. The saber blade edge faces front. Attach the back of the saber onto the left arm. Press down the palm of the [right] hand, with the five fingers extended to the front. Separate both feet in a fixed stance, with a distance equal to the width of the shoulders. (See Illustration #1.)

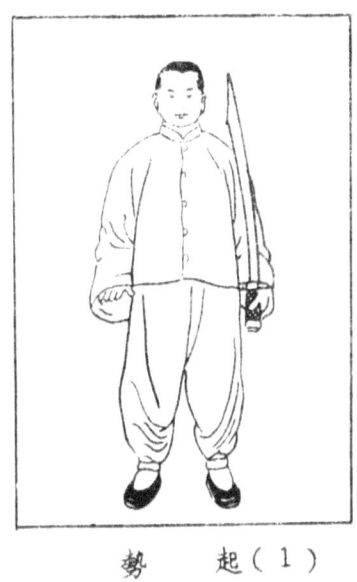

勢　起 (1)

Internal Instructions
Suspend the head and hold the body erect.
The eyes gaze levelly towards the front.
Hold the tongue against the palate and close the lips and teeth.
Inhale and exhale through the nose.
Sink the shoulders and suspend the elbows.
Relax the waist and coccyx.

The body is tranquil and the spirit relaxed.
Sink the qi gently into the Dan Tian.
Raise the spirit of vitality until it is substantial on top
    of the head.
Keep the whole body relaxed and open.
This stance is entirely like the *Beginning Posture* of Taijiquan.

2. Step Up to the Seven Star
上步七星,
Shang Bu Qi Xing
Face North

Posture Instructions
(Face towards the front.) Both hands follow the waist, turning to the left from inside and moving out until reaching the front of the chest. The back of the saber is attached to the left arm. The right hand forms a fist, with the left hand lower and the left wrist striking out to the front.

  At the same time, the right foot advances one step forward onto the heel. The left foot then follows forward with the gesture, with the toe kicking levelly to the front. (See Illustration #2.)

Internal Instructions
Retain a light and sensitive energy on top of the head.
Hollow the chest and raise the back.
Sink the shoulders and suspend the elbows.
Keep the Tail Gateway centered and upright.
The spirit of the eyes gazes to the front.

Application
The left hand and saber handle block and open the opponent's weapon. The right fist strikes their heart region. The left foot kicks against their kneecap or shinbone.

Chen Kung's Comment
Whether facing front, facing left, or facing right, the movements here can equally be used starting from any direction. This is also the case with the *Beginning Posture*. The body must maintain the proper sequence whether moving forward, backward, left, or right.

Translator's Note
1. Chen Kung is saying it doesn't matter which direction you face when starting, as the following postures will maintain the same sequence of movements. As I mentioned in the sword section, just assume that whatever direction you are facing when you start the exercise is north and proceed through the rest of the saber form accordingly.

3. Turn Left to the Seven Star
左轉七星,
Zuo Zhuan Qi Xing
Face West

Posture Instructions
(Face towards the left.) The left foot follows the waist in a leftward turn [to the west]. When reaching the left side, put the foot down on the ground. Both hands simultaneously open equally to the left and right. As soon as the entire body is facing the left side [west], bring the arms inward to enclose the internal. The right fist returns beneath the left wrist and strikes out to the front. The back of the saber remains attached to the left arm.

Simultaneously, the right foot returns to kick levelly to the front. (See Illustration #3.)

星七轉左(3)

Internal Instructions
Retain a light and sensitive energy on top of the head.
Hollow the chest and raise the back.
Lower the shoulders and suspend the elbows.
Keep the Tail Gateway centered and upright.
The spirit of the eyes gazes to the front.

Application

The opponent is coming to strike your left side. Put your body in a left turning motion. The saber handle reaches out to open up the opponent's weapon. The right fist strikes the opponent's heart region, while the right foot simultaneously kicks the opponent's shinbone.

4. White Crane Cooling Its Wings
白鶴涼翅,
Bai He Liang Chi
Face West

Posture Instructions

The right foot moves back, withdrawing until it is one half step behind the left foot, where it is put on the ground and seated firmly. The left foot follows this gesture and moves back slightly with the heel raised, ending in an Empty Stance. Both hands follow the waist and legs in a low squatting gesture. The left hand faces down; the right hand (changing into an open palm) faces up.

Simultaneously, both hands open and separate. The back of the saber remains attached to the left arm, ending just like in *White Crane Cooling Its Wings* posture [Taijiquan solo form].

Do not separate the hands with too much distance between them. (See Illustration #4.)

Internal Instructions
Retain a light and sensitive energy on top of the head.
Hollow the chest and raise the back.
Draw in the Tail Gateway.
Adhere the qi to the back of the spine.
The spirit of the eyes gazes to the front.

Application
The saber handle stirs up [撩, liao] the opponent's weapon. The right fist quickly strikes the opponent's face. The left foot simultaneously kicks the opponent's lower extremities.

5. Turn Body and Conceal the Saber
轉身藏刀,
Zhuan Shen Cang Dao
Face West

Posture Instructions
(Circle around to the right to face the left [west].) The left leg is raised slightly up; the ball of the right foot is directly on the ground. The entire body turns rightward, and while turning, is moved

into a low squatting position [Horse Stance] until it has completed one half of a circle (180 degrees). The right hand then grasps the saber handle, with the saber blade edge facing out. The entire body then turns to the right and when completing the turn, rises up and is then facing the original direction [west]. (Turn first one half circle, then complete the circle.)

The right leg, when completing the circle, rises gradually up. The right hand, holding the saber, is brought rightward and drawn in levelly. The left hand adheres to the back of the saber. The saber is held horizontally below the right kneecap. The left knee is slightly bent. (See Illustration #5.)

Internal Instructions
Retain a light and sensitive energy on top of the head.
Hollow the chest and raise the back.
The spirit of the eyes gazes to the front.

Application
First use the gesture of concealing and then draw the saber blade into the opponent's body or arm. After this, conceal the saber and prepare for the opponent to attack.

6. Push the Saber at a Slant
斜推刀, Xie Tui Dao
Face Northwest

刀 推 斜 (6)

Posture Instructions
(Face towards the left side.) The right hand and saber move toward the right, drawing the saber levelly until almost entirely upright. Turn over the wrist so the saber blade edge faces upwards. The left hand moves to the back. Move downward to chop [砍, kan]. The right foot moves one step to the right corner and is set onto the heel. This ends in a diagonal Bow Stance. The saber follows the waist and legs when moving towards the right. When moving forward, push out the saber, bringing it upwards. (This is slicing [剗, chan].)

Simultaneously, the left hand adheres to the back edge of the saber. The body moves slightly to the right corner [northwest]. The deportment of this gesture is diagonal. (See Illustration #6.)

(Regarding directing movement to the corner and joining with the previous posture, this relates to the saying: "Following each posture, you can turn and do this type of push.")

Section Two: Tai Ji Saber

Internal Instructions
The body must not be stooped too far forward.
The Tail Gateway must be centered and upright.
The spirit of the eyes gazes to the right corner.

Application
First chop [砍, kan] the incoming opponent's body from behind on the left side. Next, move forward, face the right corner and slice [刬, chan] the opponent's hand or wrist, or their body (trunk). (After slicing, slip upwards [滑, hua] with the saber to cleverly whirl out the opponent's weapon.)

7. Stir Up to the Left
左撩,
Zuo Liao
Face West

撩　　　左（7）

Posture Instructions
The left foot moves forward and across to the left, up one half step.
Follow this movement by slightly dragging the right foot forward in a "follow step." The right hand and saber follow the waist and legs and make a leftward turning gesture. When facing to the left, the right wrist turns over, so that the saber

123

blade edge faces up. From below, move upwards so to face left [west] and stir up [撩, liao] to the front. The left hand faces the back, separated and open. Both legs end in a diagonal Bow Stance gesture. (See Illustration #7.)

Internal Instructions
Relax the waist and coccyx.
Hollow the chest and suspend the head.
Hold the right elbow slightly down, without being too straightened.
The spirit of the eyes gazes at the top of the saber tip.

Application
An opponent is coming in from the left side to split [劈, pi] with their saber. In accordance with this, cross step and turn the waist so to stir up [撩, liao] with the saber's blade edge (or parry [刮, gua]), to the opponent's hand and wrist. (After parry, you can then turn over the wrist to strike with the saber blade edge to the opponent's throat.)

8. Stir Up to the Right
右撩, You Liao
Face West

撩　右 (8)

Posture Instructions
(Face towards the left.) The right foot moves to the right crosswise and forward one half step. (The left foot follows this movement and is dragged slightly forward.) The right hand and saber follow the waist and legs with a rightward turning gesture. When facing right, turn over the wrist. The saber blade edge then faces upwards. Facing the right, from below move the saber upwards. Facing forward, stir up [撩, liao] directly to the front. The left hand follows this movement and is attached to the right wrist. Both legs end in a completed diagonal Bow Stance gesture. (See Illustration #8.)

Internal Instructions
Relax the waist and coccyx.
Hollow the chest and suspend the head.
Hold the right elbow slightly down, without being too straightened.
The spirit of the eyes gazes at the top of the saber tip.

Application

From the right side an opponent uses their saber to split [劈, pi]. In accordance with this, cross-step and then turn the waist. Stir up [撩, liao] (or parry [刮, gua]) with the saber's blade edge to the opponent's hand and wrist.

Stirring up [撩, liao] to the left after turning to face right, the opponent is then the object of your stir up and turns right to avoid your attack. You must, in accordance with this gesture, turn over the hand and wrist and perform stir up [撩, liao]. Step up and with the saber's blade edge, slice [剗, chan] the opponent's stomach or arm.

Chen Kung's Comment

After performing *Stir Up to the Right*, make a forward leftward step and do *Stir Up to the Left* again. Then do another *Stir Up to the Right*. When practicing these gestures, you can repeat both sets of them two, four, or six times [ending with the right style].

9. Push the Saber Forward
正推刀,
Zheng Tui Dao
Face West

Posture Instructions
(Face towards the left.) Following *Stir Up to the Right*, turn over the right wrist so the saber blade edge faces upward. The saber follows the waist and legs in a leftward turning gesture. After the body is facing the left side, from above move down to chop [砍, kan] or split [劈, pi], splitting on line with the ribs. The right foot moves forward and slightly across.

Next, bring the left foot up [follow and sliding step], ending in a completed Bow Stance. The saber blade edge faces outward. The left foot moves forward, advancing a step in accordance with this gesture. Both hands (the palm of the left hand attached to the back of the saber) bring the saber from below and move it upwards, so that it faces forward and to the front, pushing to intercept [截, jie]. (See Illustration #9.)

Internal Instructions
Suspend the head so the Tail Gateway is upright, without too
   much stooping forward.
Hollow the chest and raise the back.
The spirit of the eyes gazes to the front.

Application

First chop [砍, kan] or split [劈, pi] to the left side and back towards the body of the incoming opponent. Again, bring the body forward and turn until facing directly forward, reaching to support the opponent's weapon, or pushing it in to intercept [截, jie] to their wrist, or slice [剗, chan] their stomach. After pushing to intercept, you can then twist out the opponent's weapon.

Connect this with the previous gesture of *Stir Up to the Right*. When the opponent is the object of your stirring up [撩, liao], this is the time to move back and withdraw to yield. You then can avail yourself of this gesture by bringing your saber back and then stepping forward to attack their side.

10. Jade Maiden Weaving at the Shuttles
玉女穿梭,
Yu Nu Chuan Suo
Face East

Posture Instructions
(Turn to face towards the right.) In joining this with the previous gesture, push the saber [outward] with both hands. The saber follows the waist and legs in a clockwise turning movement;

when facing right (bind the saber around the head with the saber tip pointing downward). At the same time the heel of the right foot is raised upwards slightly, with the sole of the foot turning completely to the right. The entire body looks just like a sparrow turning its body around. When turning completely around to the back [east], with the right hand embracing the saber at chest level (and the saber blade edge facing upwards), the palm of the left hand is then attached to the back of the saber handle. The left foot rises up. Both hands then simultaneously open and separate at shoulder level, just like in *Single Whip* of the solo form. (The saber blade edge, in accordance with this movement, turns downward. See Illustration #10.)

Internal Instructions
Retain a light and sensitive energy on top of the head.
Hollow the chest and raise the back.
The body faces slightly to the right.
The spirit of the eyes gazes forward.

Application
The saber is concealed from the opponent to all four sides, which utilizes a gesture of falsely being defective. This causes the opponent to be caught unawares. Turn the body and stab the opponent's throat or heart. The left-hand palm strikes out diagonally to the left side to another incoming attacker.

11. Drawing the Bow Levelly
平拉, Ping La
Face East

拉　　平 (11)

Posture Instructions (Face towards the right.) The left foot is placed directly on the ground. The saber tip is brought down, with the back of the saber facing up, and follows the waist and legs in a leftward turning gesture. From this downward position, move the saber upwards. Stir up [撩, liao] diagonally towards the left, reaching the level of the forehead. Turn over the right wrist, with the saber tip moving rightward, and the saber blade edge facing outward. Advance a step to the right [east]. Turn over the right wrist and move the saber tip to the left with the saber blade edge facing outward and with the left hand attached to the back of the saber. Follow the waist and legs of this gesture by moving rightward and pressing forward to *Drawing the Bow Levelly* [right style], carrying it in the hands. (See Illustration #11.)

When finishing *Drawing the Bow Levelly*, turn over the right wrist, with the saber tip moving right and saber blade edge facing outward. Step forward with the left foot. Move forward and left to *Drawing the Bow Levelly* [left style]. After

Drawing the Bow Levelly, Left Style, step forward with the right foot and return to perform *Drawing the Bow Levelly*, Right Style. (You can do these three times, five times or seven times [as long as you conclude with the right style].)

Internal Instructions
The whole body must be centered and upright.
Draw in the Tail Gateway.
Hollow the chest and raise the back.
Do not lean the body forward.
The intrinsic energy [jin] should be without the slightest obstruction.
The spirit of the eyes gazes forward.

Application
With the back of the saber, stir up [撩, liao] and strike the opponent's wrist. Wait for the opponent to neutralize, then advance step and *Draw the Bow Levelly* to their body. If they again neutralize, you must join the movement by bringing the saber to the support of the right hand and bring it back to *Drawing the Bow Levelly*, Right Style.

Chen Kung's Comment
Drawing the Bow Levelly with the saber contains the same intent as clawing [掳, lu].

12. Push the Saber at a Slant
斜推刀, Xie Tui Dao
Face Southeast

刀 推 正 (9)

Posture Instructions
(Face towards the right.) On joining this with the previous posture of *Drawing the Bow Levelly, Right Style*, turn over the right wrist so that the saber blade edge faces upwards and follows the waist and legs in a leftward turning gesture.

After this, face the body towards the left side and from above, move down to chop [砍, kan] and split [劈, pi], until reaching the level of [your] left ribs. The right foot then slightly raises up, pressing forward, and is placed on the ground. The left foot follows this gesture by moving one step forward to the right corner [southeast], completing a Bow Stance. The left hand adheres to the back of the saber with the saber blade edge facing outward. The left foot then makes an advance step gesture.

The energy of the waist and legs brings the saber towards the right [southeast] corner, moving it forward by pushing it out from below to above (this is slicing [剗, chan]).

The remaining instructions are just like the text of Posture #9, *Pushing the Saber Forward*. [See Illustration #9.]

13. Turn the Body, Wind the Saber Around the Head, and Conceal the Saber
轉身盤頭藏刀,
Zhuan Shen Pan Tou Cang Dao
Face West

式刀藏頭盤身轉（12）

Posture Instructions
(Turn right to face toward the left.) The ball of the left foot is slightly raised (with the heel touching the ground). Turn completely towards the right [to face west]. The raised right foot moves slightly towards the right side and is placed on the ground. Simultaneously, the entire body turns to the right and back.

The saber follows this gesture (with the blade edge facing downward).

When facing right, move the saber downward by drawing it back towards the right hip. The palm of the left hand is attached to the back of the saber. Pressing forward to the front, strike outward. The front foot is slightly emptied.

Turn over the right wrist so the saber blade edge faces upwards (the blade edge is facing out and the left hand palm withdraws and reaches shoulder level). Follow the waist and

legs in this gesture of completely turning around; bring the
saber up until reaching the right side of the forehead.

Wind the saber clockwise around the head (with the saber
blade edge facing outwards and the left palm withdrawn),
until reaching the level of the left shoulder. Then move it
towards the right side and downwards. Bring it back by
drawing it to the right side of the pelvis. Simultaneously,
the left palm adheres to the back of the saber.

Next, move the left hand forward and strike outward.
(See Illustration #12.)

Internal Instructions
Retain a light and sensitive energy on top of the head.
Hollow the chest and raise the back.
Relax the waist and coccyx.
Naturally move with this gesture.
Draw in the Tail Gateway.
The spirit of the eyes gazes to the front.

Application
First turn the body and use the saber to attack and clear
the opponent's weapon. The left hand strikes out to the
opponent's face. Next, take the saber and wind it completely
around the head; from above move it downward to slantingly
draw in on the opponent's wrist or body. The left hand can
then strike or seize to entice. Conceal the saber behind;
quietly observe the opponent's direction of movement,
then move forward one step to attack and strike.

14. Parry to the Left
左刮, Zuo Gua
Face Southwest

刮　　　左 (13)

Posture Instructions
(Face towards the left.) Raise up the left foot, move it forward one step diagonally to the left [southwest corner]. Turn over the right wrist, with the saber blade edge facing left. Follow the waist and legs when moving to the left side by bringing the saber face up to levelly *Parry to the Left*. The left hand simultaneously adheres to the upper part of the left Pulse Gate. Both legs finish in a Cross-Step Bow Stance. (See Illustration #13.)

Internal Instructions
Avoid leaning the upper body forward and out too much.
Issue the intrinsic energy without the slightest obstruction.
Do no raise the saber past the nose.
The spirit of the eyes gazes forward.

Application
When the opponent comes to split [劈, pi] with their saber, levelly parry [刮, gua] to their wrist with the saber blade edge.

15. Fan to the Right
右搧, You Shan
Face Northwest

搧　右 (14)

Posture Instructions
(Face towards the right.) The right foot is raised up. Pressing forward, advance one step to the right corner [northwest] and turn over the right wrist so the saber blade edge faces right. Bend the right leg and straighten the left leg, and move the body into a low squatting position. The saber follows the waist and legs when moving towards the right and down to fan [搧, shan] and chop [砍, kan]. The left hand simultaneously moves to the back, openly separated (See Illustration #14.)

Internal Instructions
Suspend the head so that the Tail Gateway is upright.
The internal energy must be issued without obstruction.
Hollow the chest and raise the back.
Sink the shoulders and hang the elbows.
The whole body must be relaxed and open.
The spirit of the eyes gazes forward.

Section Two: Tai Ji Saber

Application
When you join *Fan to the Right* with the previous application of *Parry to the Left*, the opponent will drop back to yield and avoid your attack. You then avail yourself of this and step forward to fan [搧, shan] and chop [砍, kan] at their lower extremities.

Chen Kung's Comment
After *Fan to the Right*, step forward and perform *Parry to the Left*, then repeat *Fan to the Right*. Each posture can be practiced three times.

16. Push the Saber Forward
正推刀, Zheng Tui Dao
Face West

Posture Instructions
After doing *Fan to the Right*, perform *Push the Saber Forward*. See previous Posture #9. [Illustration #9.]

Internal Instructions
Suspend the head so the Tail Gateway is upright, without too much stooping forward.
Hollow the chest and raise the back.
The spirit of the eyes gazes to the front.

137

Application

First with a chopping-like motion. split [劈, pi] to the back and left side at the incoming opponent. Again, bring the body forward and turn until facing directly forward, reaching to support the opponent's weapon, or pushing it in to intercept [截, jie] to their wrist, or slice [剗, chan] their stomach. After pushing to intercept, you can then twist out the opponent's weapon.

17. Turn the Body to Conceal the Saber
轉身藏刀, Zhuan Shen Cang Dao
Face East

Posture Instructions
(Turn rightwards to face right [east].) Raise the ball of the right foot (so that the heel is touching the ground). Turn completely around towards the right. Raise the right foot, and move it slightly to the right side and put it down. Simultaneously, after the whole body has turned right [to the east], the saber also follows this gesture (with the saber blade edge facing down). Move the saber, drawing it in, towards the right side of the pelvis. The palm

of the left hand comes off from the back of the saber, moving forward and striking out. The front foot is then slightly emptied.

For the remainder of instructions, see Posture #13, *Turn the Body, Wind the Saber Around the Head, and Conceal the Saber*, and repeat winding the saber around the head and drawing in the saber. [See Illustration #12.]

18. Stir Up the Saber
撩刀, Liao Dao
Face East

式　刀　撩（15）

Posture Instructions
(Face towards the right.) Step forward with the left foot while turning over the right wrist so that the saber blade edge faces up. The waist and legs follow this forward gesture. From its downward position, move the saber up and straight to the front to stir up [撩, liao], reaching the level of the chest. The left hand adheres onto the right Pulse Gate. Both legs finish in a completed Bow Stance. (See Illustration #15.)

Internal Instructions
Retain a light and sensitive energy on top of the head.
Hollow the chest and raise the back.
Relax the waist and coccyx.
Do not lean the body forward.
The spirit of the eyes gazes forward.

Application:
The blade edge of the saber is used to stir up [撩, liao] the opponent's wrist or body.

19. Clawing Saber
招刀, Lu Dao
Face East

式 刀 招 (16)

Posture Instructions
(Face towards the right.) Step forward with the right foot; the saber follows this forward gesture of the waist and legs. Turn over the right wrist, turning the saber towards the back until reaching the level of the right side of the forehead. Next, move it forward directly ahead to cut [剁, duo] (saber blade edge facing down) until reaching the level of the chest. Move it back at a slant to the right side of the pelvis. The left hand simultaneously

Section Two: Tai Ji Saber

comes off from the back of the saber, moves forward and up to strike out (See Illustration #16.)

The remaining instructions are just like Posture #13, *Turn the Body, Wind the Saber Around the Head, and Conceal the Saber*. Again, repeat winding the saber around the head and drawing in the saber.

Application
The opponent moves toward the back to yield and avoid your attack. You then make a false motion to the back as if yielding, move forward to carry, then cut [剁, duo] and draw the saber in on their wrist or body. The left hand can then strike out, seize, or entice.

20. Stir Up the Saber
撩刀, Liao Dao
Face East

式　刀　撩 (15)

Posture Instructions
The back of the saber faces up. Following this gesture move it upwards and back in a circular manner, turning over the right wrist, so that the saber blade edge is facing outward. From this downward position, move it upwards. Press forward directly to the front, stirring up [撩, liao] until reaching the level of the chest. The left hand adheres to the

right Pulse Gate. For the remainder of instructions, see Posture #18, *Stir Up the Saber*. [See Illustration #15.]

Application
First use the back of the saber to stir up [撩, liao] and open the opponent's weapon. Next, use the saber blade edge to directly stir up [撩, liao] the opponent's wrist or body.

21. Double Leg Kick
二起腿, Er Qi Tui
Face Southeast

Posture Instructions
(Face towards the right side.) The saber, in the right hand, is handed directly to the left hand, with the back of the saber blade attached to the left arm. The left foot follows the body in an upward gesture, towards the right corner, with the toes kicking as high as possible. The right foot, as soon as the left foot is back on the ground, kicks out to the right-side corner [southeast], with the palm of the right hand slapping the backside of the right foot. [No illustration in original text].

Internal Instructions
The body is upright and the head suspended.
The toes face front. Inhale and exhale naturally.
The spirit of the eyes gazes directly to the front.

Application

The left foot falsely entices the opponent, startling them. Make use of this opening by kicking with your right foot to their stomach or jaw.

22. Step Back to Strike the Tiger Posture
撤步打虎勢,
Che Bu Da Hu Shi
Face East

Posture Instructions
(Face towards the right.) The left foot follows the right foot. Move the left foot back one half step diagonally. Simultaneously, the waist and legs rotate to the left, with both hands following this circling gesture.

From this leftward position, move the saber down, giving the impression of sinking, until it reaches the side of the pelvis. Then move it upwards until reaching the level of the forehead. Next, circle it towards the right until reaching the right side of the forehead. Again, circle leftward. (The left hand holding the saber ends in a crosswise posture, holding the saber at ear level.) The right hand gradually makes a fist, striking towards the left, crosswise, until reaching the level of the left ribs. Both legs finish in a diagonal Bow Stance. (See Illustration #17.)

Internal Instructions
The eyes gaze to the right corner.
Retain a light and sensitive energy on top of the head.
Hollow the chest and raise the back.
Center and upright the tailbone.
Relax the waist and coccyx.

Application
Stepping back is a false intent to avoid the opponent's attacking gesture. Bring the saber upwards to seize the opponent's weapon. Within this movement, strike them with your fist. Lastly, kick them with the right foot.

23. Mandarin Duck Kicking
鴛鴦腿, Yuan Yang Tui
Face Southeast

Posture Instructions
(Face towards the right side.) The right hand takes hold of the saber and the body rises up. Raise the right leg (thigh level, knee bent and foot pointing downward). Draw the back of the saber past and around the right kneecap. (See Illustration

式刀藏身轉 (5)

#5.) Put the right foot down on the ground, finishing in an Empty Stance [facing southeast]. The saber draws to the right side; turn over the right wrist so the saber blade edge faces up. The waist and legs follow this movement. Lift it until it is at the level of the forehead. Bring it towards the left, winding it around the head (blade edge facing out and left palm drawn in) until reaching the level of the left shoulder.

Next, draw it in towards the right, moving down and to the back, until reaching the right side of the hip and thigh. Simultaneously, the left palm comes off the back of the saber to the rear, striking out to the front and upwards as it does so. The right palm takes the saber levelly across to the left rib area with the back of the saber facing inwards. Bring the saber tip from the left, moving down and back, levelly across to slice [剗, chan] (this is to obstruct [攔, lan] the opponent's waist). Simultaneously, the left hand raises, towards the right, levelly across in front of the forehead. Raise the right foot, snap kicking to the right corner [southeast]. [No Illustration given in the text].

Internal Instructions
Clearly distinguish the substantial and insubstantial.
Keep the coccyx centered and upright.
The spirit of vitality is substantial on top of the head.

Application
The right foot raises up to avoid the opponent's weapon. Simultaneously, draw in the saber blade edge on the opponent's wrist or body. If the opponent avoids or yields to this, avail yourself by chopping [砍, kan] diagonally to the

front and left. Next, draw in on the opponent's wrist or body. Again, if the opponent avoids this, clears it out, and strikes your incoming weapon, you can then avail yourself of this by seizing their wrist with your left hand. Simultaneously, use your saber to crosswise cut them or obstruct them by striking their body. If they withdraw, kick them with your right foot.

24. Turn the Body, Wind the Saber Around the Head, and Conceal the Saber
轉身盤頭藏刀,
Zhuan Shen Pan Tou Cang Dao
Face Northwest

式刀藏頭盤身轉 (18)

Posture Instructions
(Turn rightward to face the right.) The right foot withdraws and is placed down, with the toes pointing to the right side [west]. The saber follows the waist and legs of this rightward gesture. Moving right, bring the saber down and levelly draw it in to the right side of the pelvis. The left hand simultaneously opens and separates towards the left. The left foot shifts slightly rightward and forward one half step. The saber is raised upwards until reaching the side of the forehead. Then wind it around the head in a leftward manner, and continue

until it reaches the level of the right shoulder. The saber blade edge faces outward and the left palm is withdrawn.

The whole body returns to circling rightward; the right foot steps out one step towards the right corner [northwest], finishing in a Bow Stance (facing the right corner in a diagonal posture). The saber returns in moving to the right, down and to the back by drawing in until reaching the right side of the pelvis. Simultaneously, the palm of the left hand comes off the back and rear of the saber, moving forward and up to strike outward (See illustration #18.)

Internal Instructions
When turning the body, be light and nimble.
Clearly distinguish the saber blade edge and the back of the saber.
Don't allow the body to lean forward.
Keep the tailbone centered and upright.
Hollow the chest and raise the back.
The spirit of the eyes gazes front forward.

Application
Draw in the saber on the opponent's wrist or body. Turn the body, clear away and draw in to the rear of the incoming opponent. Next, *Wind the Saber Around the Head* and attack openly to the opponent's weapon. Diagonally draw in to the opponent's weapon. Diagonally draw in to the opponent's wrist or body. The left hand can strike out, seize, or entice. After *Concealing the Saber* doing a false intent gesture, quietly observe their next action. Again, attack and strike out.

25. Drifting With the Current
顺水推舟,
Shun Shui Tui Zhou
Face West

(一) 舟 推 水 顺 (19)

Posture Instructions: (Face towards the left.) The left hand follows the waist and legs in a leftward turning gesture, moving to the left and up, separating and opening. The right wrist turns over, so the saber blade edge faces up. The right foot then steps to the front [west] one step. The saber, from a downward position, moves upwards to face directly to the front, stirring up until reaching the level of the nose. The left hand moves to the back on line with the shoulder, openly. Both legs finish in a Bow Stance. (See Illustration #19.)

Section Two: Tai Ji Saber

The body then turns to the left. The saber follows the waist and legs when turning and shifting. When moving left and back, chop [砍, kan] and split [劈, pi] with the saber until reaching the level of the left rib area. (See illustration #20.)

（二）舟推水順（20）

The center of balance is on the left leg. The left hand is placed directly on top of the right elbow. The eyes gaze levelly to the rear.

Step forward with the left foot. The saber blade edge faces up. Following this advance-step gesture, the left hand adheres to the back of the saber blade. From downward, move upwards and push the saber directly forward. Both legs finish in a Bow Stance, just like Posture #9, *Push the Saber Forward*. [See Illustration #9.]

刀 推 正（9）

Turn the body to the right. The saber follows the waist and legs when turning and shifting. When moving towards the right and rear, chop [砍, kan] and split [劈, pi] with the saber until reaching the level of the right rib area. The center of balance is on the right leg. The left hand separates openly on line with the shoulders and the eyes gaze levelly to the rear.

Step forward with the right foot and again stir up [撩, liao] directly to the front. After stirring up again, move left and chop [砍, kan] to the rear. After chopping, move forward and perform *Push the Saber Forward* again.

After *Push the Saber Forward*, again move right and chop [砍, kan] to the rear. After chopping, perform stir up [撩, liao]. After stirring up, again move left and chop [砍, kan] to the rear. After chopping, move forward and *Push the Saber Forward*. It does not matter how many times you repeat the above movements, as long as you conclude with *Push the Saber Forward*.

Internal Instructions
Keep the whole body light and the waist nimble.
Unite the up and down, advancing and retreating movements.
The hand follows the saber; the saber follows the waist and legs.
To turn a complete circle, retain a light and sensitive energy on top of the head.
Hollow the chest and raise the back.
Center the Tail Gateway and keep it upright.
Gaze intently in accordance with the movements.

Application

Stepping forward to the front, stir up [撩, liao] the opponent's wrist or body. Moving left, chop [砍, kan] from behind and to the rear at the incoming opponent. Next, step forward, carry to raise the opponent's weapon and push. Moving toward the right, chop [砍, kan] to the rear at the incoming opponent behind you. These gestures are for concealing and protecting the whole body; the movements of pressing forward are for the use of attacking.

26. Turn the Body to Conceal the Saber
轉身藏刀,
Zhuan Shen Cang Dao
Face East

轉身盤頭藏刀式 (12)

Posture Instructions
(Turn rightward to face right.) Raise the ball of the right foot (so that the heel is touching the ground). Turn completely around towards the right. Raise the right foot, and move it slightly to the right side and put it down. Simultaneously, after the whole body has turned right [to the east], the saber also follows this gesture (with the saber blade edge facing down). Move the saber,

drawing it in, towards the right side of the pelvis. The palm of the left hand comes off from the back of the saber, moving forward and striking out. The front foot is then slightly emptied.

For the remainder of instructions, see Posture #13, *Turn the Body, Wind the Saber Around the Head, and Conceal the Saber,* and repeat winding the saber around the head and drawing in the saber. [See Illustration #12.]

27. Step Forward and Stir Up the Saber
上步撩刀, Shang Bu Liao Dao
Face East

Posture Instructions (Face towards the right.) Step forward with the left foot while turning over the right wrist so that the saber blade edge faces up. The waist and legs follow this forward gesture. From its downward position, move the saber up and straight to the front to stir up [撩, liao], reaching the level of the chest. The left hand adheres onto the right Pulse Gate. Both legs finish in a completed Bow Stance. (See Illustration #15.)

Internal Instructions
Retain a light and sensitive energy on top of the head.
Hollow the chest and raise the back.
Relax the waist and coccyx.
Do not lean the body forward.
The spirit of the eyes gazes forward.

Application:
The blade edge of the saber is used to stir up [撩, liao] the opponent's wrist or body.

28. Leap and Cut With the Saber
跳步剁刀,
Tiao Bu Duo Dao
Face East

Posture Instructions
(Face towards the right.) The saber follows the waist and legs in a rightward [east] turning gesture, dropping down until reaching the level of the right side of the waist, and drawing back until beside the right side of the pelvis. The left hand simultaneously presses forward, opening widely.

Then raise up the right foot, move forward and step crosswise one half step. The left foot, availing itself of this movement, jumps forward one step. The saber follows this advance stepping as the body moves into a squatting position. When moving forward, slice [剗, chan] directly downward. Both legs end in a Bow Stance. (See Illustration #21.)

Internal Instructions
Do not lean the body too far forward.
Retain a light and sensitive energy on top of the head.
Keep the tailbone centered and upright.
The spirit of the eyes gazes directly at the saber.

Application
In joining this with the previous posture of *Step Forward and Stir Up the Saber*, the opponent moves back and avoids your stirring up [撩, liao] gesture. You then avail yourself of this and leap forward to slice [剗, chan] and chop [砍, kan] to their body.

29. Energetically Split Open Mt. Hua
力劈華山,
Li Pi Hua Shan
Face South

山　華　劈　力（22）

Posture Instructions
(Face towards the back.) The saber follows the waist and legs in a rightward turning gesture and the body moves into a low squatting posture. When moving right, bring the saber from above and then directly downward to split [劈, pi] until reaching the level of the shoulder. The left hand simultaneously opens widely on line with the shoulder. Both legs end in a Horse Stance. (See Illustration #22.)

Internal Instructions
Suspend the head so the coccyx is upright.
Relax the waist and pelvis.
Hollow the chest and raise the back.
Gaze directly at the tip of the saber.

Application
Turn the body to the back, chop [砍, kan] and split [劈, pi] at the incoming opponent.

30. Embrace the Saber and Slash
抱刀剌,
Bao Dao La
Face West

Posture Instructions
(Slightly facing towards the back [south], carry [the saber] to the left [west].) As the body moves leftward and rises up, the right leg is raised, with the knee bent and toes hanging downward. The center of balance is then on the left leg. Both hands simultaneously move inward and join together, so the right elbow and right knee are on line with one another. The palm of the right hand faces inward and the saber's blade edge faces upwards to the front at a slant, with the tip pointing down. The left hand is attached to the saber handle. (See Illustration #23.)

式　刀　抱 (23)

Section Two: Tai Ji Saber

Both the left and right hands simultaneously open and separate. The right hand, holding the saber, moves directly downward to pierce [扎, zha]. The left hand moves back and up, separating openly. The right

式 刀 刺 (24)

foot simultaneously kicks outward. The body moves slightly forward and down, bending slightly. (See Illustration #24.)

Internal Instructions
Retain a light and sensitive energy on top of the head.
Keep the tailbone centered and upright.
Relax the waist and coccyx.
Hollow the chest and raise the back.
Lower the shoulders and hang the elbows downward.
Gaze at the saber tip.

Application
First avoid and yield to the opponent's weapon (or draw in on the opponent's wrist with the saber blade edge). Next, pierce [扎, zha] to the front. The right foot can follow this movement and kick the opponent's lower extremities.

31. Turn the Body Over, Change Step, and Chop
轉身換步砍,
Zhuan Shen Huan Bu Kan
Face North

式刀砍步換身翻(25)

Posture Instructions
(Face towards the front.) The right foot steps across and is placed on the ground. The body turns over and circles towards the right side. The left foot faces the right side after jumping forward (change step) one step. Bend the left knee and lower the body into a squatting position. The right leg then straightens. Simultaneously, the saber follows the turning gesture of the body. First, move the saber towards the right and up, then move it down and to the left, chop [砍, kan] across [to the west] until reaching the level of the right knee. The left hand is attached on top of the back of the right wrist Pulse Gate. (See Illustration #25.)

Internal Instructions
Do not lean the body too far forward.
Suspend the head so it is upright.
Keep the Tail Gateway upright.
The internal energy must be issued without obstruction.
The spirit of the eyes gazes at the saber blade.

Application

Turn the body to obstruct [攔, lan] and clear away the opponent's weapon. Then carry their saber to seize it, and chop [砍, kan].

32. Withdraw the Saber Posture
收刀勢, Shou Dao Shi
Face North

Posture Instructions

The body moves up with the weight divided equally on both feet (having the knees and pelvis area at first slightly bent. Afterwards, rise and straighten them). The saber follows the rightward [east] turning gesture of the waist and legs.

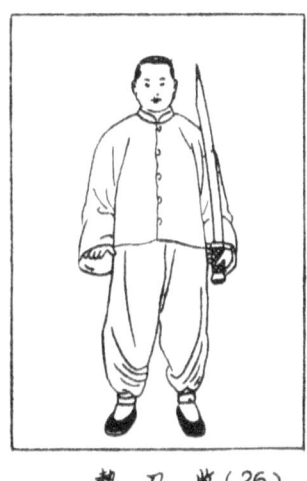

勢 刀 收 (26)

Moving right, face forward [north] until the saber reaches the level of the right side of the forehead. Then move the saber leftward and encircle it around the head (with the back of the saber facing down) until reaching the left side of the forehead. Then drop it down directly into the center of the palm of the left hand, so that the back of the saber blade is attached to the left arm. Both feet join at shoulder width's distance and the body then rises up. Both hands hang down. (See Illustration #26.)

Internal Instructions
Same position as the *Beginning Posture*.
The qi is restored to the Dan Tian.
Gather the qi to invigorate the spirit.

Pause in this stance for a short time, allowing the qi and blood to mobilize back to its origin and be restored, and then stop.

(This *Withdraw the Saber Posture* must end up on the same spot as the *Beginning Posture*, and the feet must not be separated too far apart. When practicing this, the withdrawing step is the same as that of *Drifting With the Current*. These can be either separated or matched to continue on.)

Tai Ji Saber Form Gestures

1. Beginning Posture 115
2. Step Up to the Seven-Star 116
3. Turn Left to the Seven-Star 118
4. White Crane Cooling Its Wings 119
5. Turn Body and Conceal the Saber 120
6. Push the Saber at a Slant 122
7. Stir Up to the Left 123
8. Stir Up to the Right 125
9. Push the Saber Forward 127
10. Jade Maiden Weaving at the Shuttles 128
11. Drawing the Bow Levelly 130
12. Push the Saber at a Slant 132
13. Turn the Body, Wind the Saber Around the Head, and Conceal the Saber 133
14. Parry to the Left 135
15. Fan to the Right 136
16. Push the Saber Forward 137
17. Turn the Body to Conceal the Saber 138
18. Stir Up the Saber 139
19. Clawing Saber 140
20. Stir Up the Saber 141
21. Double Leg Kick 142
22. Step Back to Strike the Tiger Posture 143
23. Mandarin Duck Kicking 144
24. Turn the Body, Wind the Saber Around the Head, and Conceal the Saber 146
25. Drifting With the Current 148
26. Turn the Body to Conceal the Saber 151
27. Step Forward and Stir Up the Saber 152
28. Leap and Cut With the Saber 153
29. Energetically Split Open Mt. Hua 155
30. Embrace the Saber and Slash 156
31. Turn the Body Over, Change Step, and Chop ... 158
32. Withdraw the Saber Posture 159

Section Three
Tai Ji Binding Staff
太極扎桿

Chen Kung's Introduction

Within Taijiquan is the Binding Staff [太極扎桿, Tai Ji Za Gan], commonly referred to as "Sticking and Adhering Staff" or "Thirteen Postures Staff," which incorporates thirteen secret characters [meanings]:[1]

1. Kai 開 (Opening)
2. He 合 (Closing)
3. Beng 崩 (Snapping)
4. Pi 劈 (Splitting)
5. Ci 刺 (Jabbing)
6. Dian 點 (Pointing)
7. Za 扎 (Binding)
8. Bo 撥 (Removing)
9. Liao 撩 (Stirring)
10. Zhan 纏 (Coiling)
11. Dai 帶 (Carrying)
12. Hua 滑 (Slipping)
13. Jie 截 (Intercepting)

Staff kung fu is very important within the Taijiquan system, as it makes use of the intrinsic energies [勁, jin] of Sticking [沾, Zhan], Adhering [黏, Nian], Neutralizing [化, Hua], Closing [合, He], Enticing [引, Yin], and Issuing [發, Fa]. These energies are identical to those within the empty-hand styles [of Sensing Hands, 推手, Tui Shou] and are equally as subtle and extraordinary.

The training procedure for the staff is divided into two categories: solo drilling and two-person sparring sets. To reach a level of great skill in either of these categories, however, takes a long time. The staff should be thought of as if it were the hand. The intrinsic energy of the entire body must be able to pass through the staff directly to the tip, just as if it was mercury filling a tube. When issuing the intrinsic energy, it must be gathered at the rear of the staff and issued to the tip.

The training procedures of the staff and its practical uses are likewise embodied in two other weapons, the halberd and long spear. At present, some practitioners use the long spear only, but this is truly a mistake as it means they have not yet understood the true function of the staff in relation to Taijiquan.

Who was it that authored the names of the postures and styles of the Yang family staff? Yang Luchan. He once put out a fire with his staff (to save a building). His reputation was truly wonderful.

When two staffs meet, no matter if seizing or thrusting is being employed, it is the same as using the empty hand. When joining with the opponent's staff in sparring, slip away so as to be independent of them, then strike with the staff as though thrusting with the hand. Frequently, this principle is misunderstood, yet it is fundamental to this profound kung fu.

The ancient historical traditions of this art are presently lost in the past, however, we can still examine and practice the methods. The exercises are divided into solo staff gestures, two-person circular sticky staff, and two-person active step (four staff techniques of jabbing the heart, leg, shoulder and throat), also there are numerous movements contained within the thirteen secret styles. Furthermore, these divisions were handed down by the Yang family descendants, which enabled this great and wondrous national treasure to remain intact.

The staff is a waxed stick made of rattan that is grown in both Honan and Shandong provinces. These are flexible yet very strong and are not easily cracked or broken. Formerly, the staff was but the handle for the spear and halberd.

Rattan staffs are of two types: dark and light. The light colored staffs are preferable because of their rings (knot joints). Among the most desirable are those that grow thirteen feet or longer, having rings along the length of them. The initial three feet should be without rings, but the upper length should have rings about every three feet. Each of these sections is then designated yin or yang. These staffs are completely natural and are the very best. The more rare dark-colored rattan staffs are reddish. These are like beautiful antiques and are also considered the more readily usable staff, but nowadays they are seldom seen.

To acquire the secrets of this art, you must excel with continuous practice for well over one year.

Translator's Notes
1. The meanings and uses of Taiji Binding Staff's *thirteen secret characters* are found within the instructions of the staff postures themselves. The applications of these thirteen meanings are quite varied, just as are the Thirteen Posture secret meanings of Taijiquan. These

applications run from coarse applications to the very subtle, and are correlated with the Thirteen Postures of Taijiquan. As in the Taijiquan empty-hand form, and the sword and saber forms, Advancing, Withdrawing, Looking-Left, Gazing-Right, and Central Equilibrium are aspects of how the Eight Postures and their corresponding staff characters (one through eight in the list below) function. So Warding-Off (or Opening), for example, can function in any of the Five Operations (nine through thirteen in the list), and this is true for the other seven postures and their staff equivalents. So it is not a simple matter of looking at or describing these thirteen secret characters as purely individual techniques.

1. Warding-Off relates with Opening.
2. Rolling-Back with Closing.
3. Pressing with Snapping.
4. Pushing with Splitting.
5. Pulling with Jabbing.
6. Splitting with Pointing.
7. Elbowing with Binding.
8. Shouldering with Removing.
9. Advancing with Stirring.
10. Withdrawing with Coiling.
11. Looking-Left with Carrying.
12. Gazing-Right with Slipping.
13. Central Equilibrium with Intercepting.

From these correlations you can see that Opening, for example, can function in the operations of either

Stirring, Coiling, Carrying, Slipping, and Intercepting (as these equate with the Five Operations of body movements).

Single-Person Binding Staff Method
單人扎桿法, Dan Ren Za Gan Fa

The solo staff techniques within Taijiquan are simple to perform, comprising three movements in two sequences:

> One: Opening [開, Kai], Closing [合, He], and Thrusting [發, Fa]:
> This drill is practiced for incoming strikes that are above the waist, and the thrust is directed straight out at chest level.
>
> Two: Removing [撥, Bo], Closing [合, He], and Thrusting [發, Fa]:
> This drill is practiced for incoming strikes that are below the waist, and the thrust is directed diagonally downward at knee level.

When practicing, position the left foot so it is directly toward the front. The right hand holds the rear of the staff and the left hand is placed midway from the center. The feet are separated in a Bow Stance that more resembles a Horse Stance (or "T" stance).[1] The entire body should be relaxed and loosened, with a light and sensitive energy retained on top of the head.

Section Three: Tai Ji Binding Staff

First Solo Drill
Kai, He, and Fa[2]
開合發

Opening [開, Kai]: The right hand sinks downward as the left hand slides upward along the staff. The tip of the staff is moved upward and to the left. The weight simultaneously shifts onto the right leg. Gaze intently at the tip of the staff. (See Illustration #1.)

（式 開）桿 扎 人 單（1）

Application
When the opponent's weapon approaches your body is the time to use opening [開, kai].

Closing [合, He]: Both hands move to be in line with the waist, by directing the staff downward into closing [合, he]. Within closing [合, he], there is a small clockwise circling gesture. The backside of the left hand has now turned over and faces up and the right palm turns to face upward. So, from opening [開, kai], return to the original posture with equal weight on both legs. Gaze intently at the staff tip. (See Illustration #2.)³

(式 合) 桿 扎 人 單 (2)

Application
When the opponent's weapon approaches your body use this pressing down motion.

Section Three: Tai Ji Binding Staff

Thrusting [發, Fa]: Keeping in accordance with the above gestures, the right hand follows the movement of the waist and legs by pressing forward to thrust [發, fa] with the staff. The right-hand Tiger's Mouth faces forward and the left hand remains stationary as the staff slides smoothly through the center of the palm when it is thrust outward. In other words, it is the right hand that thrusts the staff in actual application; the left hand only supports the staff within the palm. At this time the majority of the weight is shifted onto the left leg, but not entirely because it's not advantageous when you need to change or neutralize into a withdrawing gesture (always guard against this before taking the initiative). Gaze intently at the staff tip. (See Illustration #3.)[4]

(式 發) 桿 扎 人 單 (3)

Application
This is a jab [刺, ci] or piercing motion to the opponent's pit of the stomach, throat, or shoulder.

171

Second Solo Drill
Bo, He, and Fa
撥合發

Removing [撥, Bo]: The left hand sinks and slides downward along the staff, as the right elbow and hand are raised to ear level. The tip of the staff is moved diagonally downward and to the left. The weight simultaneously shifts onto the right leg. Gaze intently on the tip of the staff. [See Illustration 1B.]⁵

Application
When the opponent's weapon approaches your lower body is the time to use removing [撥, bo].

Section Three: Tai Ji Binding Staff

Closing [合, He]: Both hands move to be in line with the waist, by directing the staff downward into closing [合, he]. Within closing [合, he], there is a small clockwise circling gesture. The backside of the left hand has now turned over and faces up and the right palm turns to face upwards. So, from removing [撥, bo], return to the original posture with equal weight on both legs. Gaze intently at the staff tip. [See Illustration 2B.]⁶

Application

When the opponent's weapon approaches your body use this pressing down motion.

Thrusting [發, Fa]: Keeping in accordance with the above gestures, the right hand follows the movement of the waist and legs by pressing forward to thrust [發, fa] with the staff. The right hand Tiger's Mouth faces forward and the left hand remains stationary as the staff slides smoothly through the center of the palm when it is thrust outwards. In other words, it is the right hand that thrusts the staff in actual application; the left hand only supports the staff within the palm. At this time the majority of the weight is shifted onto the left leg, but not entirely because it's not advantageous when you need to change or neutralize into a withdrawing gesture (always guard against this before making the initiative). Gaze intently at the staff tip. [See Illustration 3B.]⁷

Application
This is a jab [刺, ci] or piercing motion to the opponent's knee.

Chen Kung's Comments on Solo Staff
Essential points for performing Thrusting [發, Fa]:

Be as if suspended from above so that the body is held perfectly erect.

Hollow the chest and raise the back.

Sink the shoulders and suspend the elbows.

Seat the waist and sink the qi into the Dan Tian.

Make use of the intrinsic energy entirely from the waist and legs, not from the hands, otherwise you will not be able to exhibit a shaking motion in the staff. This is as though the hands were hardly even considered in actual application. So when issuing out the intrinsic energy the entire body must be involved, from the foot into the leg, into the waist and then to the spine, then into the shoulders and on into the hands so that the energy penetrates through to the very tip of the staff. When thrusting out the staff, the intrinsic energy begins at the rear of the staff as it is issued from the body. It then goes straight through the staff to the tip, causing a shaking motion as if mercury traversed the center.

After performing thrusting [發, fa], withdraw back into opening [開, kai] and return to closing [合, he]. Henceforth, these postures should be performed repeatedly in a circular manner.

Chen Kung's Comment
The staff illustrations within this material are only drawings. Consequently, they must be examined carefully for any imperfections.

Translator's Notes
1. Make a T stance by standing in a wide Horse Stance with feet online with each other, then turn out one foot to the side direction. This then makes the stance resemble a "T."
2. Opening (Kai), Closing (He), and Thrusting (Fa) and Removing (Bo), Closing, and Thrusting can also be thought of as neutralize, seize, and attack, which are the movements governing Sensing Hands and Dispersing Hands techniques. These three movements actually become one in application, so that in one circular motion all three movements are joined.

With this type of solo staff technique, it is very easy to increase the level of intrinsic energy, not like that of the Shaolin School with the many Plum Blossom styles of staff. Only through pure experience and serious practice can this intrinsic energy be developed, but this is no easy matter. Therefore, on no account carelessly disregard practice!

The left style has the right foot forward and left hand thrusting the staff. The right style has the left foot forward and the right hand thrusting the staff. Both of these are identical in execution. Alternate training the left and right hands, as both sides must be developed. Otherwise, one hand will be weakened and unable to balance the strength of the body.

Within Chinese boxing, it is essential that the empty hand forms be practiced to improve the muscles. Weapons serve to improve sinews and bones. Through repeated practice of Taijiquan empty-hand

style, you can attain all the fundamental standards. Subsequently, weapon practices like the sword, saber, and staff will take you even further in skill. At this point you will find it difficult to not practice.
3. In Illustration 2, the index finger does not belong on top of the staff as shown, rather it should be held loosely below.
4. In Illustration 3, the staff should be held at mid-chest level, not at neck level.
5. Chen Kung did not include illustrations for the Second Solo Drill, so these images were taken and modified from other exercises. Illustration 1B, for example, shows the move you would make in Removing (Bo).
6. This version of Closing (He), 2B, is the same as in the First Solo Drill.
7. Thrusting (Fa), 3B, is the same as in the First Solo Drill, except this modified illustration shows that the thrust is to the lower body (knee) of the opponent and not to the chest.

Two-Person, Level-Circular Sticking and Adhering Binding Staff
雙人平圓沾黏扎桿法
Shuang Ren Ping Yuan Zhan Nian Za Gan Fa

This method develops Sticking [沾, Zhan] energy. Practicing this two-person staff technique is the basis and foundation for the kung fu of this energy, which embodies the three energies of Opening [開, Kai], Closing [合, He], and Thrusting [發, Fa]. The usefulness of these three energies is truly great. Furthermore, they aid in the heating of the "gate of life" [the kidneys] in our bodies, which in turn nourishes the energy of Issuing [發, Fa]. The results and benefits of these staff techniques are equal with those of both Circular and Fixed Sticky Sensing-Hands exercises.

Jabbing the Shoulder
This method is divided into four gestures of attack: jabbing [刺, ci] the shoulder, throat, heart, and leg. But this particular method makes use of just the shoulder, heart, and throat attack gestures, whereas the jabbing [刺, ci] to the leg is the second exercise of this method.

To Begin:
Both men stand facing opposite one another. In the drawings, A is the darkened image and B the lighter image. Each hold their staff while having their left foot forward so that they both can perform thrusting [發, fa] with their right hand. A initiates the action by jabbing [刺, ci] to B's left shoulder.

Section Three: Tai Ji Binding Staff

B avails himself to the incoming attack, protecting himself by bringing his staff upward into opening [開, kai]. At this point, B's opening [開, kai] gesture seizes all of A's incoming force, and B changes into closing [合, he]. (See Illustration #1.)

(１)雙人平圓沾黏扎桿法(刺肩式)

After performing closing [合, he], B then jabs [刺, ci] to A's left shoulder. A then neutralizes this attack with opening [開, kai] and then seizes B's staff with a closing [合, he] gesture, after which B directly proceeds to thrusting [發, fa].

Both men apply opening [開, kai], closing [合, he], and thrusting [發, fa] alternately. Both men alternate the jabbing [刺, ci], first to the shoulder, then the heart, and lastly to the throat, doing so in a rotating and repetitive manner without interruption or pause.

Now, if the right foot is in front then the left hand will thrust [發, fa] the staff, in the same fashion as would the right hand. Only in this case, the left style, the jab [刺, ci] is to the opponent's right shoulder, then the heart, and throat. When jabbing [刺, ci] outward, the thrusting [發, fa] should be done with the two hands extended outward in an arc and slightly separated on the staff, with one hand in front and the other at the rear of the staff.

Jabbing the Leg
This method is divided into two styles: Fixed Stance and Active Step.

Fixed Stance Drill
Both men stand opposite one another. Each practitioner has the left foot forward. A initiates by jabbing [刺, ci] at B's left knee. B then avails himself of the incoming attack by moving his staff slightly downward and to the left with a removing [撥, bo] gesture. Simultaneously, B raises his left foot slightly to evade A's piercing jab [刺, ci]. When the majority of A's force is exhausted, B then in a likewise manner jabs [刺, ci] at A's left knee. (See Illustration #2.)

（式腿刺）法桿扎黏沾圓平人双（2）

When A is the object of B's jab [刺, ci], he moves his staff downward at a leftward angle into a removing [撥, bo] gesture. Simultaneously, A raises his left foot slightly to evade B's piercing jab [刺, ci]. Both men perform removing [撥, bo] and jabbing [刺, ci], jabbing and removing, reciprocating alternately in this manner.

Active-Step Drill[8]
This exercise remains obedient to the above drill (Fixed Stance).

B performs removing [撥, bo] and raises his left foot slightly as A directs a jab [刺, ci] to B's left knee. B then steps over and across one step to the right with the left foot. The right foot then "follow steps," whereupon B then likewise jabs [刺, ci] at A's left knee. A then performs removing [撥, bo] with his staff and slightly raises his left foot. A then steps over and across one step towards the right with the left foot. The right foot then follow steps, whereupon A again jabs [刺, ci] at B's left knee.

Both men rotate in this manner to complete an entire circular figure, so that with each change of stepping there is a removing [撥, bo] gesture and with each jab [刺, ci] there follows a removing gesture. Both circle around in this fashion without interruption.

Now with the right foot forward, the left hand will perform thrusting [發, fa] and jabbing [刺, ci] in the same manner as the right hand (this is the left style). Both players must mutually alternate left and right styles of the staff during these circular patterns.

This kung fu of jabbing [刺, ci] to the shoulder and then the knee will become increasingly more profound with repeated practice. The circling gestures of the staff will become ever smaller, without any pauses and when both staffs make contact there will be little or no sound. In contrast, if the circling remains too big, the resulting kung fu will be shallow.

Translator's Note
8. In the active-step drill, each player should step in such a manner so as to position their self in each of the eight directions. For example, when A steps from facing east into facing northeast, B must then step from facing west into facing southwest, and so forth.

Two-Person, Fixed Standing Circular Form, Sticking and Adhering Binding Staff Method
雙人立體圓形沾黏扎桿法
Shuang Ren Li Ti Yuan Xing Zhan Nian Za Gan Fa

[Two-Person Cornering Circular Sticky Staff]
The Circular Sticky Staff (with Active Step) method is not entirely complete; this exercise supplements it. If you only do the Active Step and not the Fixed Stance, there will, consequently, be an insufficiency in application and it will be easier for an opponent to gain an advantage.

Drill Method
Both men stand opposite one another and each has their left foot forward. A then jabs [刺, ci] at B's left knee. B avails himself of the incoming attack by raising his left leg while simultaneously moving his staff downward into a leftward angle removing [撥, bo] gesture. (See Illustration #1.)

一之法桿扎黏沾形圓體立人雙（１）

When A's force is exhausted, B circles his staff upwards and around into a closing [合, he] gesture. (See Illustration #2.)

二之法桿扎黏沾形圓體立人雙（2）

A is then the object of B's jab [刺, ci]. A then does removing [撥, bo] and then performs closing [合, he] by winding around his staff, moving upwards and around in one complete circle. A then jabs [刺, ci] at B's left knee. B must then raise his left leg as A jabs [刺, ci] and must also simultaneously repeat a left-side removing [撥, bo] gesture, and again circling upwards and around into closing [合, he].

Summary

When A jabs [刺, ci], B neutralizes with removing [撥, bo], [seizes with] closing [合, he], and attacks with jabbing [刺, ci]. A will then perform removing [撥, bo] to neutralize, closing [合, he, to seize], and thrusting [發, fa] to attack, and so forth.

If the right foot is in front, the left hand does the jabbing [刺, ci]. This is exactly the same in execution as the right-hand style, except in this case the jabs [刺, ci] are to the right knee.

Chen Kung's Comment
A high level of skill is needed for executing this technique of completely winding the staff around into a closing [合, he] gesture. Being able to perform carry [帶, dai] and enjoin the opponent's staff back and out so to create a separation is just like the Sensing-Hands energies of Issuing [發, Fa] and Intercepting [截, Jie], having the same marvelous application.

Two-Person, Active-Step, Four Staff Methods of Jabbing the Heart, Leg, Shoulder, and Throat
雙人動步刺心刺腿刺肩刺喉四桿法
Shuang Ren Dong Bu La Xin La Tui La Jian La Hou Si Gan Fa

This Four Movement Staff Method has the same meaning as Active Step Sensing-Hands. Both seek to rotate the upper and lower parts of the body to neutralize and attack, with the body motion as one complete unit. Training in the hands, body, and stepping methods is very important, but this can only be accomplished empirically—and even this is not easy. Training must certainly be diligent if the skills of this profound and wonderful kung fu are to be attained. Also, the principles of this Four Movement Staff Method cannot be thoroughly reasoned without comparison to the subtle principles of Sensing Hands.

Preparation: Both practitioners stand opposite one another and each has his left foot forward.

Jabbing the Heart

A first takes a step by withdrawing the weight onto the right foot and then stepping out one half step with the left foot. The right foot then follows and steps forward. A then jabs [刺, ci] at B's heart [actually the solar plexus], and B simultaneously withdraws his right foot and retreats one half step. The left foot then follows backwards accordingly. B then performs an opening [開, kai] gesture and closing [合, he] gesture as A's staff approaches. (See Illustration #1.) [A is facing west and B is facing east.]

一之法桿四扎步動人雙（1）

Jabbing the Leg

A, being the object of B's seizing gesture, steps forward and diagonally right with his right foot. The left foot then follow steps, so that the body ends facing the corner [southwest]. Simultaneously, A makes a withdrawing circle [clockwise] with his staff and then jabs at B's left knee.

B withdraws his left foot and draws it near his right foot. His staff moves down and to the right into a removing [撥, bo] gesture and then executes closing [合, he] to A's staff. (See Illustration #2.) [A faces southwest and B faces northeast.]

二之法桿四扎步動人雙（2）

Section Three: Tai Ji Binding Staff

Jabbing the Shoulder

A, now being the object of B's removing [撥, bo] and closing [合, he] gestures, steps forward with the left foot, which is then followed by the right foot, so that he is directly opposite B. A then circles his staff upwards and to the right (clockwise) and proceeds to jab [刺, ci] at B's left shoulder. B, subjected to A's jab [刺, ci], withdraws by stepping to the right and back, with the left foot, circling his staff upwards and into a closing [合, he] gesture as A's staff approaches his body. (See Illustration #3.) [A faces south and B faces north.]

Jabbing the Throat

A, again being the object of B's closing [合, he] gesture, again steps forward with the left foot to the right while the staff moves in a circular motion towards the right and back (clockwise). This motion is to both open [開, kai] and neutralize B's staff. A then jabs [刺, ci] B's throat, making B the object of A's jab [刺, ci]. B then withdraws by stepping to the right and bringing back the left foot. At the same time he circles his staff completely around to execute a closing [合, he] gesture to A's approaching staff. (See Illustration #4.) [A faces southeast and B faces northwest.]

雙人動步扎四桿法之四 (4)

Changing Positions
The remaining postures are the same as above. A has now changed roles and is now performing the previous B side, and B has likewise changed to do the A side. When B finishes the four-movement staff jabs, he again changes to neutralize and withdraw, and A also changes to advance and attack. Both men alternate the drilling of withdrawing and advancing.

Chen Kung's Comment
With a united effort both players must train to learn the techniques of the waist and legs, hands and feet, the advance and withdraw methods, neutralize and attack, so that the staff work of both partners is in unison and is without sound or pause. This is to attain excellence in the use of the staff.

When practicing, you must pay attention so as to not obstruct the intrinsic energy, while also retaining a vibrant spirit of vitality and ensuring nimble and active movement without any awkwardness or interruption to the form. The whole body must be centered and upright. Hollow the chest and raise the back. A light and sensitive energy must be retained on top of the head, and the qi should rise and fall so that it adheres to the spine and sinks down into the Dan Tian.

The conditions of the above principles must be put into practice, as they are the training fundamentals for all the staff methods. Additionally, even after continued training, the order of these movements should not be altered: always jab [刺, ci] to the heart, leg, shoulder, and throat.

In conclusion, whether attacking or neutralizing, advancing or retreating, follow the above principles without fail.

Tai Ji Binding Staff Forms

Binding Staff Solo Drills 168
    First Drill 169
        Kai (Opening) 169
        He (Closing) 170
        Fa (Thrusting) 171
    Second Drill 172
        Bo (Removing) 172
        He (Closing) 173
        Fa (Thrusting) 174

Two-Person Circular Sticking-and-Adhering Binding Staff 178
    Jabbing the Shoulder, Heart, and Throat 178
    Jabbing the Leg 180
        Fixed-Stance Drill 180
        Active-Step Drill 181

Two-Person Cornering Circular Sticky Staff 183

Two-Person Active-Step Four-Movement Staff Method 186
    Jabbing the Heart 187
    Jabbing the Leg 188
    Jabbing the Shoulder 189
    Jabbing the Throat 190

About the Translator

Stuart Alve Olson, longtime protégé of the Taijiquan Master T.T. Liang (1900–2002), is a teacher, translator, and writer on Daoist philosophy, health, and internal arts. Since his early twenties, he has studied and practiced Daoism and Chinese Buddhism.

As of 2013, Stuart has published eighteen books, many of which now appear in several foreign-language editions. He is currently working on completing the entire Chen Kung Series with revised editions of earlier works as well as new volumes on sections he has never previously published.

Stuart has performed numerous book signings, appeared on many TV and radio talk shows throughout the United States, written several articles for martial art and Daoist magazines, and has taught Daoism and Taijiquan in Taiwan, Hong Kong, Indonesia, Canada, and Italy.

Stuart was voted the 2012 *IMOS Journal* Reader's Choice Award for "Best Author on Qigong."

He currently lives in Phoenix, Arizona, with his wife, Lily.

Brief Biography

On Christmas Day, 1979, Stuart took Triple Refuge with Chan Master Hsuan Hua, receiving the disciple name Kuo Ao. In 1981, he participated in the meditation sessions and sutra lectures given by Dainin Katagiri Roshi at the Minnesota Center for Zen Meditation. In late 1981, he began living with Master

Liang, studying Taijiquan, Daoism, Praying Mantis Kung-fu, and Chinese language under his tutelage.

In the spring of 1982 through 1984, Stuart undertook a two-year Buddhist bowing pilgrimage, "Nine Steps, One Bow." Traveling along state and county roads during the spring, summer, and autumn months, starting from the Minnesota Zen Meditation Center in Minneapolis and ending at the border of Nebraska. During the winter months he stayed at Liang's home and bowed in his garage.

After Stuart's pilgrimage, he returned to Liang's home to continue studying with him. He and Master Liang then started traveling throughout the United States teaching Taijiquan to numerous groups, and continued to do so for nearly a decade.

In 1986, Stuart published his first four books on Taijiquan— *Wind Sweeps Away the Plum Blossoms*, *Cultivating the Ch'i*, *T'ai Chi Sword, Sabre & Staff*, and *Imagination Becomes Reality*.

In 1987, Stuart made his first of several trips to China, Taiwan, and Hong Kong. On subsequent trips, he studied massage in Taipei and taught Taijiquan in Taiwan and Hong Kong.

In 1989, he and Master Liang moved to Los Angeles, where Stuart studied Chinese language and continued his Taijiquan studies.

In early 1992, Stuart made his first trip to Indonesia, where he was able to briefly study with the kung-fu and healing master Oei Kung Wei. He also taught Taijiquan there to many large groups.

In 1993, he organized the Institute of Internal Arts in St. Paul, Minnesota, and brought Master Liang back from California to teach there.

In 2005, Stuart was prominently featured in the British Taijiquan documentary *Embracing the Tiger.*

In 2006, he formed Valley Spirit Arts with his longtime student Patrick Gross.

In 2010, he began teaching for the Sanctuary of Dao and writing for its blog and newsletter.

In 2012, Stuart received the *IMOS Journal* Reader's Choice Award for "Best Author on Qigong."

Body of Works
Taijiquan
  Chen Kung Series
   Tai Ji Qi: Fundamentals of Qigong, Meditation, and Internal Alchemy, Vol. 1 (Valley Spirit Arts, 2013).
   Tai Ji Jin: Discourses on Intrinsic Energies for Mastery of Self-Defense Skills, Vol. 2 (Valley Spirit Arts, 2013).
   Tai Ji Quan: Practice and Philosophy of the 108-Posture Solo Form, Vol. 3 (Valley Spirit Arts, forthcoming).
   Tai Ji Tui Shou & Da Lu: Mastering the Eight Operations of Sensing Hands and Greater Rolling-Back, Vol. 4 (Valley Spirit Arts, 2014).
   Tai Ji San Shou: Dispersing Hands Exercises for Mastering Intrinsic Energies Skills, Vol. 5 (Valley Spirit Arts, forthcoming).
   Tai Ji Bing Shu: Mastering the Arts of Sword, Saber, and Staff Weapon Skills, Vol. 6 (Valley Spirit Arts, 2014).
  Other Taijiquan Books
   Tai Ji Quan Treatise: Attributed to the Song Dynasty Daoist Priest Zhang Sanfeng (Valley Spirit Arts, 2011).
    (Daoist Immortal Three Peaks Zhang Series)

Steal My Art—The Life and Times of Tai Chi Master T.T. Liang (North Atlantic Books, 2002).

T'ai Chi According to the I Ching—Embodying the Principles of the Book of Changes (Healing Arts Press, 2002).

T'ai Chi for Kids: Move with the Animals, illustrated by Gregory Crawford (Bear Cub Books, 2001).

Imagination Becomes Reality: 150-Posture Taijiquan of Master T.T. Liang (Valley Spirit Arts, 2011).

The Wind Sweeps Away the Plum Blossoms: Yang Style Taijiquan Staff and Spear Techniques (Valley Spirit Arts, 2011).

T'ai Chi Thirteen Sword: A Sword Master's Manual (Unique Publications, 1999).

Daoism

The Jade Emperor's Mind Seal Classic: The Taoist Guide to Health, Longevity, and Immortality (Inner Traditions, 2003).

Tao of No Stress: Three Simple Paths (Healing Arts Press, 2002).

Qigong Teachings of a Taoist Immortal: The Eight Essential Exercises of Master Li Ching-Yun (Healing Arts Press, 2002).

Kung-Fu

The Complete Guide to Northern Praying Mantis Kung Fu (Blue Snake Books, 2010).

Forthcoming Daoist Books by Stuart Alve Olson

Refining the Elixir: The Internal Alchemy Teachings of Daoist Immortal Zhang Sanfeng
(Daoist Immortal Three Peaks Zhang Series)

The Immortal: The True Story of Li Qingyun, the 250-Year-Old Man—1678 to 1936 by Yang Sen.

The Book of Sun and Moon: Traditional Perspectives on the Book of Changes (Yi Jing)

Check out Stuart's author page at Amazon:
www.amazon.com/author/stuartalveolson

Chen Kung Series

From the Private Family Records of Master Yang Luchan

A Master's Program on the Art of Taijiquan

Tai Ji Quan, Sword, Saber, Staff, and Dispersing Hands Combined,
by Chen Kung
太極拳刀劍桿散手合編, 陳公著
Tai Ji Quan Dao Jian Gan San Shou He Lun,
Chen Gong Zhe

Without question, of all the Taijiquan literature produced in the past three hundred years, none has surpassed or equaled the depth of Chen Kung's work. Foremost in Taijiquan literature, Chen's book, first published in 1936, is a distinct and invaluable resource, providing teachings from the Yang family private transcripts.

Covering the traditional Yang family system of Taijiquan practice and philosophy, translations with commentary of the entire text are now being presented to English readers in this new multi-volume series by Stuart Alve Olson.

No matter what style of Taijiquan you practice or what level of expertise you have achieved, this series of books will greatly broaden your knowledge and skills, as it is truly a "Master's Program" on the art of Taijiquan.

Tai Ji Qi: Fundamentals of Qigong, Meditation, and Internal Alchemy (Vol. 1) provides the foundational teachings for developing the internal energy of qi through traditional Yang family Qigong and meditation practices. This volume provides all the information needed for beginning studies on Taijiquan. A companion instructional DVD is available from Valley Spirit Arts.

Tai Ji Jin: Discourses on Intrinsic Energies for Mastery of Self-Defense Skills (Vol. 2). This text provides a full list with explanations of each intrinsic energy trained through Taijiquan practices. The information contained within this volume is unquestionably some of the most valuable and rare writings on Taijiquan.

Tai Ji Quan: *Practice and Philosophy of the 108-Posture Solo Form* (Vol. 3) focuses on the instructions for the Yang-style solo form, Taijiquan history, Taijiquan classical texts, and the practical applications for each posture. This volume provides invaluable information for any style of Taijiquan.

Tai Ji Tui Shou & Da Lu: *Mastering the Eight Operations of Sensing Hands and Greater Rolling-Back* (Vol. 4) focuses on the initial two-person exercises to develop the yielding and sensing energies that make Taijiquan so effective in practical application.

Tai Ji San Shou: *Dispersing Hands Exercises for Mastering Intrinsic Energies Skills* (Vol. 5). Dispersing Hands is the apex two-person practice for developing the Taijiquan solo form applications, Sensing Hands, and Greater Rolling-Back intrinsic energies skills.

Tai Ji Bing Shu: *Mastering the Arts of Sword, Saber, and Staff Weapon Skills* (Vol. 6) focuses on the Taijiquan weapons. Sword, saber, and staff further develop the expression of intrinsic energies through the arms (via the sword), through the spine (via the saber), and through the waist and legs (via the staff).

Along with the detailed translation work of Stuart Alve Olson, each volume provides in-depth, clear, and insightful commentaries from what he learned through his years of study with Master T.T. Liang (1900–2002), one of the greatest Taijiquan masters of our time.

About the Publisher

Valley Spirit Arts offers books and DVDs on Daoism, Taijiquan, and meditation practices primarily from author Stuart Alve Olson, longtime student of Master T.T. Liang and translator of many Daoist-related works.

Our website provides teachings on meditation and internal alchemy, taijiquan, qigong, and kung fu through workshops, private and group classes, and online courses and consulting.

For more information about us as well as updates on Stuart Alve Olson's upcoming projects and events, please visit:

www.valleyspiritarts.com

About the Sanctuary of Dao

The Sanctuary of Dao is an online educational center featuring articles, translations of Daoist texts, a Daoist Book Club, weekly Dao Talks, and a Daoist Calendar.

We also offer weekly meditation sessions and seasonal meditation retreats in Phoenix, Arizona.

Please visit our website at www.sanctuaryofdao.org for more information about our organization and programs.

www.ingramcontent.com/pod-product-compliance
Lightning Source LLC
Chambersburg PA
CBHW030652230426
43665CB00011B/1058